Sul Revival

Saladin, His Greater Syria, & Its Echoes in the Modern Middle East

S. A. Murad

Contents

A Tribute to My Family and Syria

1154 Map of the World

Introduction

Part I   THE ASCENDANT (1137 - 1169)

     1. Something May Come of Him

     2. The Eastern Cross

     3. 1099

     4. The Calling

     5. A Knife's Edge

     6. Masters

Part II   THE SULTAN (1169 - 1177)

     7. By Will of the Pen

     8. David's Descendants

     9. Two Sultans

     10. Tremors in the Land

     11. Uniting the Realm

Part III   THE LIBERATION (1177 - 1187)

     12. Shattered

13. Reversing the Wind

14. The Raider

15. A New King

16. The Horns

17. The Opening

Map of the Salahuddin's Dominion

19th-century Ottoman Drawing of Masjid Al-Aqsa

Mosaics from the Umayyad Mosque, Damascus, Syria

Old City of Damascus Oil Painting

16th-century Ottoman Painting of Aleppo

1555 Map of Cairo by Piri Reis

19th-century Ottoman Painting of Mecca

19th-century Ottoman Painting of Masjid An-Nabawi

1537 Ottoman Painting of Istanbul

Part IV   THE SIEGE (1187 - 1191)

18. The Victor's Burden

19. The Gathering Storm

20. At the Walls of Acre

21. Bone and Iron

22. Waves of Fire

23. Besieged

24. The Fall

25. Massacre

Part V   THE PREVAIL (1191 - 1193)

26. Blood Never Sleeps

27. The Struggle

28. The Warrior Sultan

29. The Return

30. The Revival

Epilogue - The Modern Middle East

Appendix

A Tribute to My Family and Syria

"In the name of God, the Most Gracious, the Most Merciful."

    I must take this moment to express my sincere gratitude to those who have supported me in the long journey of creating this book. First and foremost, I extend the deepest appreciation to my mother and father (may Allah bless them), who gave me the gift to travel at a young age and see the world for all the beauty it contains. Travel was the best education they provided me with, and truly it is the most rewarding, profound, fulfilling, and exhilarating lesson one can experience in life. From Latin America to Europe and the Middle East, every flight on the plane, every drive in the car, and every walk in the street has shaped my perspective and enriched my appreciation for the diversity of the world and everything that makes us human.

I must also dedicate this book to my grandparents (may Allah bless them). Every word of Arabic and every story about our country I learned from my grandparents. It was with them that I experienced Syria for the first time when we traveled there in the summer of 2023. Due to the civil war that ravaged the country, I have lived most of my life in America without ever having been to Syria, until, when the situation became suitable, my grandparents used the opportunity to offer me the best gift any Syrian could ask for, which is to see their homeland.

My family (may Allah bless everyone of them) comes from Damascus, from a neighborhood called *Rukn Al-Din*. It is in this district in the north of the city that I stayed for the summer. It has long been known as the Kurdish quarter of Damascus, for the excellent people who reside there and for the fact that it was originally named after Ruknuddin Mankuris Al-Faliki Al-Adili, a servant to the half-brother of Al-Adil, the brother of Sultan Salahuddin. The neighborhood of Rukn Al-Din possesses another connection to the legendary sultan, whom it is the mission of this book to explore. Just a few blocks away from my family's apartment is the Salahuddin Mosque, one of the main centers of the community, where the people gather every Friday to pray. Its construction was due in part to the financial support of my great-grandfather, Muhammad Bassim Murad (may Allah rest his soul), who was, in many ways, a pillar of the community and a well-known voice in the old Syria.

Muhammad Tawfik Murad Pasha   Muhammad Bassim Murad

Born in 1911, as the son of Muhammad Tawfiq Murad Pasha, an Ottoman government official and military officer, my great-grandfather grew up to witness the French occupation of Syria. The presence of the French in Syria led him to start his career as a journalist, advocating for independence from France. Syria won this independence on April 17th, 1946. His newspaper would come to be known as *Al-Akhbar*, "The News." In the 1960s, Syria's political environment underwent dramatic turmoil with the rise of the Ba'ath Party and the eventual creation of the infamous regime of Hafez Al-Assad, when he rose to power in 1971.

My great-grandfather had made it his career, as a journalist and the owner of one of the most read newspaper companies in Damascus, to speak out and use his voice to enjoin good and condemn evil. Known for its outspoken views against numerous governments, his newspaper was initially shut down first by Gamal Abdel Nasser's administration when Syria merged with Egypt in the union of 1958 and then by the Ba'ath Party in 1963. With the rise of Hafez Al-Assad and his crackdown on what remained of Syria's once independent press, my great-grandfather, perhaps as one of the earliest targets of the regime, was forced into hiding by the suppressive state, until the order for his arrest was lifted through family connections. Many Syrians, however, had it far worse. Muhammad Bassim Murad (may Allah rest his soul) passed away in 1975, around the age of 64.

Now in the year 2025 and in light of Syria's liberation, it is my duty to write this book, not simply to draw from our history and offer lessons to the new Syria, but also to use our freedom of speech in this time when the Syrian perspective has once again become center stage. For 53 years of suppression by the state, the voices of millions of Syrians have been silenced. And in the 13 years of destruction caused by the civil war, there is not a single person who has not suffered from it, directly or indirectly, by the loss of their loved ones, their homes, their livelihoods, or even their mental health.

The scars we endured as people will take years to heal.

But if we have survived through these years, then I believe we can transcend the pain. It can transform us and give us the power to overcome anything in this world. This is the true blessing of being Syrian, that we know what true resilience and determination looks like. Now with the country freed and whole again, our nation must prevail in these early days of reconstruction. And as there exist a number of voices in the global media that attempt day and night to slander the leadership of the new Syrian government or worse morally exonerate the crimes of the old regime, the voice of the Syrian people now matters more than ever, as we take these crucial steps into the future to rebuild and reclaim the country we lost.

Murad 10

1154 Map of the World by Muhammad Al-Idrisi

Introduction

Dirham of Salahuddin (1215 - 1216)

In Dante's *Inferno*, the famous 14th-century Italian poem, there is a special place in Hell, just above the deepest, most wretched circle, where Europe's non-Christian heroes are acknowledged. Here, in this first circle of Hell, virtuous men like Socrates and Aristotle are placed besides the likes of Homer, Hector, and Julius Caesar, existing in limbo, outside of God's salvation. Interestingly, Dante places a single Muslim ruler amongst these European men. His name was Salahuddin Yusuf Al-Ayyubi—*Saladin*. While the Europeans of Dante's time did not waver in their condemnation of Islam, Salahuddin was a figure so exceptional in character, chivalry, and nobility that even a writer like Dante could not ignore his virtue and reject him to the worst of Hell. He was placed alongside the great heroes of the European imagination not as a villain, but as a man of honor.

But unlike many of Europe's most celebrated, Salahuddin was not born of a special lineage. He was not the son of a king, nor the heir to a kingdom. His family neither came from wealth nor power. He was not even the most physically impressive warrior. He was, in many ways, an ordinary man, a human. And yet, by the end of his life, he was one of the most revered leaders in both the Muslim and Christian worlds, not merely for his conquests, but for his exemplification of the chivalry of the Sunnah of the Prophet Muhammad ﷺ.

To the Europeans, Salahuddin was a manifestation of a code of honor they scarcely believed could exist in the foreign adversary that was the Muslim world. To the Muslims, he was a leader who commanded their trust and loyalty, who would open the doors of Jerusalem once more. But beyond his reputation as the liberator of the holy city, Salahuddin carried another vision, one often overlooked. He sought not just the restoration of Jerusalem but the revival of Greater Syria, Bilad Al-Sham.

Before delving any further, it is necessary to make the distinction between two terms that will be of central focus in this book. The *Levant* is the word given to describe the region of the Middle East, touching the eastern Mediterranean, that encompasses the modern countries of Lebanon, Palestine, Jordan, and of course Syria. This land is also known in the Arab and Muslim world as *Bilad Al-Sham*, and in the West more famously as *the Holy Land*. The Levant is defined by diverse topography, from coastal green valleys and even snow-capped mountains in the west to arid expanses of desert in the east.

Culturally, the Levant has been a place touched by the influences of numerous peoples throughout history. The Canaanites, Jews, Phoenicians, Arameans, Philistines, Egyptians, Assyrians, Babylonians, Persians, Greeks, Romans, Arabs, Latins, Turks, Circassians, Chechens, Bosniaks, Kurds, Druze, Armenians, and Western Europeans have all left their mark here. Cities like Beirut, Tripoli, Latakia, Haifa, Jaffa, and Gaza rise on its coast, while Homs, Hama, Aleppo, Amman, Raqqa, and several others rest in the heartland, with Damascus and Jerusalem existing at the center of the religious imagination of the people of the land and for many others throughout the world.

But in stark contrast to the Levant, Bilad Al-Sham, or the Holy Land, *Greater Syria* is a very different word, whose weight carries not only geographical and cultural significance, but more especially a profound political idea. Greater Syria is more than a region; it is a vision for a single, unified state that transcends modern borders and asserts itself as a dominant regional power, leading the direction of the politics of the Middle East on the global stage.

The last time that Syria stood at the center of the Muslim world was during the height of the Islamic Empire under the Umayyad Caliphate. From Damascus, the capital of their state, the Umayyads ruled a dominion that stretched far beyond Syria. It spanned across three continents, from the shores of the Atlantic in Spain to the edges of China in Central Asia. This was Islam's era of military conquest and territorial unity, an age of expansion and governance unmatched in its scale and magnitude. Not even the Romans built a realm so large as this. It was from Syria that the caliphate became the largest empire that the world had yet known.

Thus, it was not by mere chance that Salahuddin made Damascus the capital of his state. Syria was not just strategically essential. It was and *is* the chosen land. The Prophet Muhammad ﷺ himself, who once visited Syria as a child, praised it as the land of the righteous and "Allah's chosen land, to which His best servants will be gathered" [Sunan Abi Dawud 2483]. The Sahaba, his companions, traveled, lived, and died there.

The graves of Bilal Ibn Rabah, Zaynab Bint Ali, and Muawiyah Ibn Abi Sufyan (رضي عنهم الله) are in Damascus. Khalid Ibn Al-Walid (رضي الله عنه), one of the greatest generals in the history of war, is buried in Homs. Tamim Al-Dari (رضي الله عنه) is in Palestine. And Jafar Ibn Abi Talib, Zayd Ibn Haritha, and Abdullah Ibn Rawahah (رضي الله عنهم) were killed in battle and are buried in Jordan, as is Abu Ubayda Ibn Jarrah (رضي الله عنه). The earliest generations of Muslims, who had witnessed the dawn of Islam, had envisioned Greater Syria as the land where faith, leadership, and destiny converged. Salahuddin sought to restore that vision, to return Greater

Syria to its former place, as the seat of strength for the Ummah.

Yet the significance of Syria was not and is not exclusive to Islam. It was, and remains, a land deeply enshrined in the Christian and Jewish traditions as well. In Palestine, it is the land of the prophets, from Abraham (عليه السلام) to Jesus (عليه السلام). In Lebanon, it is a place whose cedar trees are revered in the Bible. And in Damascus, it is where the John the Baptist, Yahya (عليه السلام), is buried. Greater Syria has always been a land where prophecy and revelation converged within one contiguous story for the followers of the Abrahamic faiths. And at the time of the arrival of the Muslims and the first centuries thereafter, all three, Muslims, Christians, and Jews, coexisted peacefully as the cousins of one community.

But by the 11th century, after years of decline and division, the land would see the gradual erosion of peace, as the various Muslim polities fought amongst themselves, often to the harm of the region's Christians. And then came the Crusades. In 1099, Jerusalem was taken. For the first time, a foreign army had penetrated so deep into the Islamic world, occupying one of its holiest places, Al-Aqsa, that the question of revival turned into a serious demand.

With Jerusalem and much of the Levant under occupation, it was Salahuddin, who emerged as the leader capable of uniting the fractured Muslims and reversing the tide. And he did so not by declaring a caliphate, nor by venturing to the distant caliphs in Baghdad, but by anchoring his power in Syria. He recognized what history had long proven, that Syria was the key to the region. With Damascus as his base, he built a state through battles, diplomacy, strategy, and an unwavering sense of purpose. He promised Al-Aqsa to the Muslims. They trusted him. And they followed him for it.

Today, in the 21st century, we watch as the same region remains as contested as ever. It is today divided in ways that mirror the division of those fractured Muslim polities of the 11th century. The modern nation states of Syria, Lebanon, and Jordan, as well as Egypt, Iraq, Saudi Arabia, and others constitute much of what once was a united region, each one with their own competing interests and political realities.

Moreover, there is a new entity that, since its inception has stood to completely reshape and upend the geopolitical landscape of the Middle East. This is the State of Israel. Its policies for the last century, particularly regarding its territorial control, have long been a source of tension for the broader region. Ardently supported by the United States and Europe, while historically resented in the Arab world by contrast, Israel has no doubt been at the center of the Middle East's political history for the last century. Its presence in the occupied areas of the West Bank and Gaza has fueled conflict, ever since these lands were seized in the wars of 1948 and 1967. Since 1967 and the wars of 1975 in Lebanon, 1980 between Iraq and Iran, the Gulf War of 1990, Iraq in 2003, the Arab Spring, and the multiple wars between Israel and Hamas, the state of the Middle East has seemed to hang at the edge of conflict, clouded with uncertainty.

But a different trend was seen on a momentous day, December 8th, 2024, in Syria, freed after a decade of civil war and over half a century of injustice under the Assad regime. And just as Syria was pivotal to Salahuddin's victory in the 12th century, it remains so to the future of the Middle East. Syria's story serves as a reminder that no status quo lasts forever. The Syrian people, who endured decades of appalling oppression and years of horrific war, proved this on December 8th, when they brought down the 50-year-old, barbaric, tyranny of the Assad regime.

The story of Salahuddin, his Greater Syria, and the Muslim revival is not a relic of the past. His vision for the region echoes into the present and perhaps even into the future as well. Today, as many analysts, statesmen, and policymakers look to develop the region, one cannot help but recognize how Syria is absent from the frame. Without Syria, such projects for a better Middle East are certain to fail. Syria is home to 23 million people with neighboring Lebanon at almost 6 million and Jordan at 11 million. This goes without even considering the forgotten 5 million Palestinians in the West Bank and Gaza. Combined, the people of this historic land number around 45 million, nearly the size of the Gulf's population of 57 million.

No policy for the Middle East region is complete without considering the people of Greater Syria, not just their presence on the map but also their rights, aspirations, and claim to equal treatment by the rest of the world. By recognizing the centrality of Syria in Salahuddin's time and ours, we gain not just an insight into history but a deeper understanding of the Middle East, not as a land of conflict but as a land of reverence among three great religions and of political resilience within its peoples, who continue still to strive for their true independence and their day of resurgence on the world stage. Just as Salahuddin's legacy shaped the region in a time of immense instability, it continues to offer perhaps the strongest perspective for studying why Greater Syria matters and why it holds the potential to matter even more in the future than we could possibly imagine. The centuries-old struggle for this land has been the longest and most driven in history. And just as in Salahuddin's time, it remains unfinished.

Part I
The Ascendant
(1137 - 1169)

Statue of Salahuddin
Kerak, Jordan

Chapter 1
Something May Come of Him

The Umayyad Mosque, Damascus, Syria

"And thus We established Yusuf in the land, to settle therein wherever he willed. We touch with Our mercy whom We will, and We do not allow the reward of the doers of good to be lost."

وَكَذَٰلِكَ مَكَّنَّا لِيُوسُفَ فِى ٱلْأَرْضِ يَتَبَوَّأُ مِنْهَا حَيْثُ يَشَآءُ ۚ نُصِيبُ بِرَحْمَتِنَا مَن نَّشَآءُ ۖ وَلَا نُضِيعُ أَجْرَ ٱلْمُحْسِنِينَ

- Surah Yusuf of the Quran (12:56)

Before he was known to the world by his honorific name, *Salahuddin* (صلاح الدين) "the Righteousness of the Faith," he was a simple, ordinary man. And his name was Yusuf. In the Quran, as it is in the Bible, it was Prophet Yusuf (عليه السلام) (Joseph), who was abandoned in a well, as a child, by his envious brothers. Many years later, these same brothers would find Yusuf once again, but as a great leader, as the ruler of Egypt. Like the prophet, whom he was named after, Salahuddin's path would also take him to the reigns of leadership. But early on in his life, it was unclear what would become of him, let alone if he would survive past infancy. Yusuf was born in 1138 or perhaps earlier in 1137, in the town of Tikrit, in Iraq, as the son of Najmeddin Ayyub.

Yusuf's lineage, from his father, Najmeddin, was actually not of Arab birth. They were Kurdish. And in fact, the vast majority of the figures that were part of the Muslim revival were not Arab either. Many of the rulers, soldiers, scholars, diplomats, and commanders were Turks, Kurds, or even Persian. But the Kurds, in the worldview of the ruling elite of the time, were seen as a lesser people to their Arab and even Turkic brethren. The Kurds never had their own distinct political entity within the first few centuries of Muslim history. No empires, kingdoms, or even heroes of the Kurds were ingrained within the imagination of the Muslim world, at least not yet.

Yusuf's mother was Sitt Al-Mulk Khatun. Very few details remain from her time to paint a picture of who she was. But one story does provide an insight. Before Yusuf was born, she reported to have had a dream while she was pregnant with him. This story, like many throughout this book, comes from Mamluk era chroniclers, over a century later in the 1300s, when it was compiled in Abu Al-Fida's *Tarikh Al-Mukhtasar fi Akhbar Al-Bashar*, "The Concise History of Humanity." In the dream, she saw, within her stomach, a sword. The sword, with all the symbolism it carried, took the form of her child. And whether or not she indeed had this dream, the profound spirit of that sword would come to shape the boy's life and define his role in the world he would enter.

Two or three years before Yusuf's birth, in 1135, the Middle East was far from what the future sultan of revival would make it to be. While the Muslims in Syria were still divided and struggled to keep the Latin Crusaders at bay, one ruler had consolidated control, where others had lost it. His name was Imaddedin Zengi, the Atabeg of Mosul and Aleppo. Imadeddin had largely inherited his authority from the remnants of the Great Seljuk Empire, which by 1135 was a shadow of its former self.

In September of that year, Sultan Mahmud II died, and the Seljuk state fell into disorder. Mahmud II, ruling over Iran and Iraq, had been a key supporter of Imaddedin's efforts in Syria. With his death, a power vacuum was set to break down whatever remained of the Seljuks. Rival governors and warlords vied for power. Sons and brothers of the dead sultan turned on each other. One claimant to the throne, Ghiyathidin Mas'ud of Fars, emerged to make his bid for his father's position. Seeing an opportunity, Imadeddin Zengi entered into an alliance with this new sultan.

Together they waged a campaign against the caliph of the time, Al-Mustarshid of the Abbasid Caliphate. The power vacuum had presented the Abbasid caliph a chance to re-exert his authority over Baghdad and the surrounding areas. Upon summoning an army, the caliph had declared his independence in an attempt to break free from his Turkic overlords. The Seljuk claimant nor the Zengid atabeg would allow it. Both Turkic leaders met the Abbasid army at Samarra, north of Baghdad. The Zengid army, already hindered by their long march into the Iraqi countryside, was routed at Samarra, sending Imadeddin and his men to retreat north, back to Aleppo and Mosul.

But during the campaign against Baghdad, Imadeddin was aided by one local leader and his Kurdish allies. Najmeddin Ayyub was governor of Tikrit at the time of the battle, placing his support behind the Zengid atabeg. When Imadeddin withdrew, Najmeddin, along with his family, followed him out of Iraq. On the very day that the family departed Tikrit, the mother gave birth, and Yusuf was born. His birth coincided with the war that was being waged in the background. Death and peril surrounded the family on all sides. And so one could say that when Yusuf entered the world, he entered it as a victim of war, as someone who was forced from his home. He was born as a refugee.

As the family traveled on the road to Mosul, some onlookers passed by and allegedly told the father, "Perhaps this baby is a bad fortune."

Given the difficult circumstances that the family was already beset with, the loss of their home and their displacement from their land, it seemed to some that the birth of a child, in the midst of all of these calamities, was not a sign of good things to come. But Najmeddin Ayyub did not share that outlook. He believed in the immense possibilities for his son, that perhaps one day, *something may come of him*.

He would reply to them, "No. Rather it may be that Allah has planned through him a blessed fortune that we cannot yet see."

Prospects for the family of Ayyub would improve with their integration into the Zengid administration. In late 1144, Imadeddin Zengi moved against the Crusaders. His target was the city of Edessa, the first Crusader state to be founded in the Levant. Both Najmeddin and his brother, Asadeddin Shirkuh, served Imadeddin Zengi during the time of the siege, albeit in lesser capacities than other figures in the Zengid circle. On Christmas Eve, December 24, 1144, Edessa fell to Imadeddin, and the Muslim recapture of the city was complete.

However, his victory over the Franks would not go unchallenged. While the atabeg continued to thwart attempts by the Crusader states to retaliate to his conquest of Edessa, it was a threat from within that led to his death. In 1146, Imadeddin Zengi was assassinated by a Frankish slave he owned, likely taken as a prisoner of war. His death would be followed by the ascension of his son, Nureddin Mahmud Zengi.

Taking advantage of the death of the atabeg, one year later, in 1147, the Crusader states: the Kingdom of Jerusalem, Tripoli, and Antioch, launched the Second Crusade. Its objective was the capture of Damascus. However, disunity within the Crusader army, poor leadership, and their inability to surmount the robust fortifications of Damascus all led to the Second Crusade ending in failure. Nevertheless, Damascus, ruled and defended by the declining Burid dynasty, was for the first time made a target of Crusader expansionism. And it was feared by many across the region that if the Crusaders returned to lay siege again, the Burids would be incapable of protecting the city, and then all of Syria would be open for Crusader attacks.

Nureddin, whose influence in the region had surpassed that of his atabeg father, had made himself and his state independent from the Seljuks. The Zengid state was his, and he ruled it as its sultan. Unlike his father, Nureddin was motivated deeply by the Islamic revivalist movement at the time, which demanded and stressed the importance of unity among the Muslims in order to defeat the Crusaders. Such a vision meant that Damascus had to be part of Nureddin's state. And so in 1154, after the death of the Atabeg of Damascus, Muineddin Unur, Nureddin set out with his army from Aleppo and captured Damascus.

For years now, the Ayyubid family had supported the efforts of the Zengids. With the addition of Damascus, Nureddin rewarded them for their commitment. The ancient town of Baalbek, just north Damascus, in present day Lebanon, was granted to Najmeddin Ayyub as a fief. It was there that the family would build their estate. In Damascus, however, Najmeddin would send Yusuf to study in the madrasas.

The madrasas, schools of Islamic education, were instrumental in the investment of the generation of Salahuddin. As division and disputes of theology and political theory crippled the Ummah for decades, the Muslims of the time turned to opening madrasas in the greater project of reviving the Muslim world and bringing forth new generations of leaders. In fact, during the 11th and 12th centuries, more madrasas were being built than were mosques, a testament to the significance that education played. At the very core of this academic movement were the essential questions that the Muslims asked themselves: "Who has the authority to interpret Islamic law? How should it be interpreted? What should Islamic governance look like? And what does it mean to be Muslim?" The first step of revival was for the Muslims to follow the purest form of Islamic orthodoxy and rediscover what they were truly about.

What made the Zengids, under Nureddin, such a unique entity, in contrast to some of its predecessors, was its consolidation of power in the form of ministers, who were classically trained in Islamic law, completed the full memorization of the Quran at a young age, served as administrators of the state, and supported the sultan towards the greater aim of one day liberating Al-Quds, the holy city of Jerusalem. These administrators, along with the sultan whom they served, came from Damascus, Aleppo, Mosul, and all across the Middle East. But the single unifying factor that made the emergence of this generation of leaders possible was the Nizamiyya school in Baghdad.

In response to the Fatimid Al-Azhar school in Cairo, the Seljuk Vizier, Nizam Al-Mulk, commissioned the construction of a number of new Sunni schools to counter the growing influence of the Ismailis of Egypt. The first madrasa of Nizam Al-Mulk was built in Nishapur, in Iran, before he eventually established the Nizamiyya Madrasa in Baghdad, becoming arguably the most influential Sunni school of its time and hosting some of Islam's most prestigious scholars with the famous Al-Ghazali being among its teachers.

Because of these schools and the intellectual power that sprung from them, a movement to revive and restore the ideology of the Sunni Muslims was gradually taking root, aiming to usher in a new era of Sunni Islamic political leadership. By the reign of Sultan Nureddin Zengi, the effects of this movement were starting to materialize. And so as

Yusuf, still as a young boy, lived in Damascus in this era of classical academic revival, he gained a deep understanding of the Quran and the Sunnah, applying it not to the mere remembrance of history, but to the political realities that surrounded him.

It was through his education that he learned more and more of the loss of Masjid Al-Aqsa, Jerusalem, and the Holy Land to the Crusaders, as well as the difficulties that prevented the Muslims from liberating it, above all was the absence of unity. Among the masses, there existed a mentality of pessimism around the idea of a freed Jerusalem, that the Muslims would never be able to reconquer the Holy Land and prevail against their adversaries. But Yusuf's worldview pointed to greater prospects. His studies took place in the beating heart of Damascus itself, Masjid Al-Umawi, the Umayyad Mosque.

Masjid Al-Umawi, built by the Umayyad Caliph, Al-Walid I, is more than a testament to the wealth of Islamic architecture. It is, in many mirroring ways to Al-Aqsa, a place that is engraved with such deep lore and history that reaches back thousands of years into the past. Around 800 BCE, it was once a temple to Hadad, a deity for rain and fertility, worshipped by early Semitic people. When Syria was conquered by Rome, in the 1st century, it became a temple to Jupiter. And with the spread of Christianity, around 500 CE, it became a church. Its connection to Jesus (عليه السلام) is so profound that not only does it still contain the tomb of John the Baptist, but it is also believed that on the White Minaret, Jesus (عليه السلام) will make his return, at the end of the world, as the Messiah.

It was in this magnificent place that Yusuf memorized the Quran, became a master of the Shafi'i school of knowledge in Islamic jurisprudence, and where he learned his first lessons on political theory and military strategy. From religion, literature, science, politics, diplomacy, and even war, Yusuf's education certainly prepared him for the world that he was about to enter and inspired him to become a great leader of the Muslim revival, just like his role model and mentor, Nureddin Zengi.

Sultan Nureddin, who also grew up with an Islamic education and a deep understanding of its role in driving forward the Muslim revival, personally taught the young Yusuf in Damascus, seeing in him a special quality that distinguished him from the rest of the students. And so Nureddin would continue to invest in and cultivate his relationship with the young boy. As the years passed, and Yusuf's knowledge and skills were refined under the mentorship of his master, he, in his teenage years, was made a soldier in the Zengid army. And not long after gaining his rank and distinction within the army, the student earned his title and was henceforth known as *Salahuddin*, "the Righteousness of the Faith."

Chapter 2
The Eastern Cross

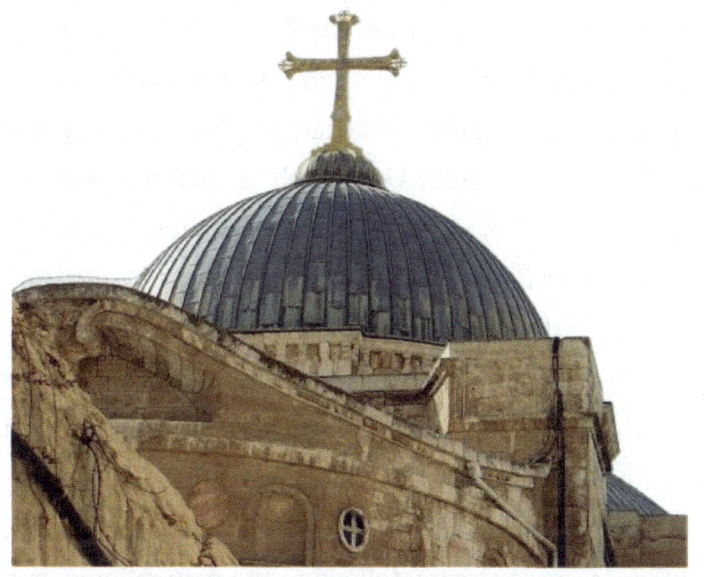

Church of the Holy Sepulchre, Jerusalem, Palestine

"You will surely find the nearest of people in affection to the believers to be those who say, 'We are Christians.' That is because among them are priests and monks, and because they are not arrogant."

لَتَجِدَنَّ أَشَدَّ ٱلنَّاسِ عَدَٰوَةً لِّلَّذِينَ ءَامَنُوا۟ ٱلْيَهُودَ وَٱلَّذِينَ أَشْرَكُوا۟ ۖ وَلَتَجِدَنَّ أَقْرَبَهُم مَّوَدَّةً لِّلَّذِينَ ءَامَنُوا۟ ٱلَّذِينَ قَالُوٓا۟ إِنَّا نَصَٰرَىٰ ۚ ذَٰلِكَ بِأَنَّ مِنْهُمْ قِسِّيسِينَ وَرُهْبَانًا وَأَنَّهُمْ لَا يَسْتَكْبِرُونَ

- Surah Al-Ma'idah of the Quran (5:82)

Before Islam's arrival in the 7th century, and even longer before Salahuddin and the Crusader states that he contested with, the land of Greater Syria had been shaped by Christianity under the rule of the Roman Empire. Before the names "Islam," or "Muslim," or "Muhammad" were ever associated with the land, Syria had long been the very heart of Christianity with cities like Antioch, Damascus, Bethlehem, Nazareth, and of course Jerusalem hosting many of Christendom's most revered places.

After the conversion of Emperor Constantine I to the Christian faith in 312 AD, the empire was subsequently Christianized. But already there had been provinces within the empire, which had previously embraced the Christian faith or at least earlier forms of it. The Coptics, Armenians, and Syriacs were already following the new religion as early as the 1st century. With Constantine's Christianity, the empire would have to navigate these preexisting elements and accommodate them under the rule of Constantinople.

The Roman or rather Greek mark on Christianity would diffuse across the empire, prominently in the Levant. Jerusalem, the city revered in the Christian tradition for Christ's crucifixion and resurrection, became a focal point for pilgrimage with travelers coming from all corners of the Greek and Mediterranean world. And by 400 AD, Christianity was *the* religion of the Levant. Its legacy was etched into the landscape through its construction of churches, monasteries, and communities that still exist to this day throughout the region.

Under Eastern Roman rule, Orthodox Christianity would emerge as the dominant faith of the East, but it did so whilst undergoing significant internal change in the process. The Christian faith's journey from strict monotheism in the Holy Land to its later form in Greek Orthodoxy was marked famously by the Council of Nicaea in 325 AD.

In the lush, mountain province of Bithynia, in modern day Iznik, Turkey, a city lying at the shores of a serene lake, a council of over 300 bishops convened at the imperial palace, arriving from Egypt, Anatolia, and of course Syria. The council was announced by Emperor Constantine, who sought to bring the Christian communities of the empire to a consensus in order to strengthen the unity of the realm. The meeting lasted for two months, almost the entire summer from May until July. After a series of fierce arguments, the Creed of Nicaea was officially adopted, giving the Church a unified doctrine and affirming the full divinity of Christ within the Trinity, a three-person god. All other, pre-Roman interpretations of the faith, such as the rejection of the Trinity by some scholars, were soundly denounced and condemned as heresy.

The traditions and elements of the Nicene doctrine would go on to shape Levantine Christianity for centuries to come, but there would still be an enduring yet dwindling presence of that pre-Roman Christianity, one with deep roots tracing back directly to Jesus (عليه السلام) and those early Christians.

Among the stories that chronicle the evolution of Christianity in the Levant is that of Salman Al-Farsi (رضي الله عنه). Originally from Iran, from where his name, *Al-Farsi*, originates, meaning "the Persian," Salman was a student of multiple religions in his lifetime. Disillusioned with Zoroastrianism, he traveled to Syria, seeking the truth and salvation that Christianity promised. And it was in Syria that he passed through the circles of various priests, each one sending him off towards teachers more righteous than the last, in pursuit of learning the purest version of Christianity, the one closest to Jesus (عليه السلام).

Islam views these generations of devout Christians with a deep sense of admiration and respect. The gap between Jesus (عليه السلام) and Prophet Muhammad ﷺ saw Christianity's message of monotheism undergo many changes. Even at the Council of Nicaea, it was Arius, the anti-trinitarian priest from Alexandria, who was branded a heretic for his beliefs. At a time when adherents to early Christian monotheism were becoming a microscopic, even ostracized sect, Muslims would later come to appreciate these believers for their commitment to following God's message in the sense that they understood as the purest form.

As for Salman, with the death of his last teacher and no other mentor alive from this diminished line, he would be guided by the advice of his master's dying words towards a land of "date palms." As it turned out, Salman would reach the city of Medina, where he met Prophet Muhammad ﷺ and embraced Islam among the ranks of the Sahaba.

But it was this diverse and nuanced tapestry of Christianity, from the debates at the Council of Nicaea to Salman Al-Farsi's exposures in Syria to remnants of early Christianity, that illustrates how complex the Christian faith was in the Levant and throughout the Middle East. Orthodox, Coptic, Armenian, Syriac, and many other communities emerged as distinct yet related families of Christianity within this period of change. And nearly all of them would be exposed to a second wave of change, albeit an external one, heralded by the arrival of the Muslims.

In the year 635 AD, Damascus was conquered by the Arab armies of Khalid Ibn Al-Walid and Abu Ubayda Ibn Al-Jarrah (رضي الله عنهم), who set out from Medina, on the orders of the Caliph Abu Bakr (رضي الله عنه). The caliph's war objectives were simple: eliminate the threat posed by the Romans, avenge the defeat of the Muslims from their first engagement with the Romans at the Battle of Mu'tah, and ultimately fulfill the Prophet's ﷺ vision of expanding the borders of Islam into Al-Sham. After a lengthy siege and months of assaulting and bombarding the walls, Damascus surrendered to the armies of the caliphate. Following their entry into the former Roman city, the Sahaba would begin to arrive and settle in the country. And the vast majority of them would never leave, remaining buried there to the present day.

With the arrival of the Islamic faith and the transition of rule from Roman Christian to Arab Muslim, the majority composition of the Levant's demographic character would in fact remain Christian. Islam would only gradually diffuse into the population, a religious osmosis that would take many years for it to actually become the leading religion. In the first few centuries of caliphate rule, the Christian citizens, paying of course the jizya tax, would continue to occupy various functions of urban and rural life, as merchants, academics, scribes, translators, and even advisers to the caliph.

Much of what is known from this time period comes from Syriac accounts. In contrast to Greek and Latin outlooks on the Islamic world, which were almost always entirely from a place of antagonism, given the wars fought in Anatolia, Spain, and the Mediterranean, Syriac accounts present more mixed attitudes with some more positive than others. The participation of Syriac and, more broadly, Eastern Christians in the development of the Islamic world underscores the value attached to them by their Muslim rulers and neighbors.

In fact, many of the achievements of the Islamic Golden Age were made possible because of the efforts and skills of Christians within the caliphate. Because of translators of Greek medical and philosophical texts like Hunayn Ibn Ishaq, Yuhanna Ibn Masawayh, Abu Bishr Matta Ibn Yunus, and perhaps even Al-Kindi himself, as he may have belonged to some Christian heritage, the Islamic Golden Age should be better described as the Arab Golden Age. It was a period of development, reflecting such religious diversity, wherein not everyone was Muslim, but everyone certainly knew Arabic, as that was the language of academia and broader society.

Truly, it was the collaboration of the caliphate's most skilled individuals, belonging to both Christian and Muslim backgrounds alike, that was responsible for producing, translating, and preserving some of the most remarkable advancements of the time as well as those of past civilizations. This was the pinnacle of the relationship between Christians and Muslims in the Islamic world.

And then came the decline and the Crusades.

Chapter 3
1099

Statue of Pope Urban II in Clermont, France, pointing eastward

Within the story of Salahuddin, the fact that Jerusalem was lost in the first place, points to an evident trend of decline in the Muslim world. And it was this vulnerability that allowed the Crusade to be so successful in carving out portions of the Holy Land for the Latin and Frankish entities. But this great decline, however, was set in motion by a long line of developments that predate the events of 1095, when the Crusade was first declared by Pope Urban II in the town of Clermont, in France.

In the 11th century, the Islamic world, from Cordoba to Baghdad, was thrown into an abyss of fire, the epitome of a civilization's decline, plagued by deepening rivalries and great division amongst its many rulers. The authority over the Muslims, now held by the Abbasid Caliphate, deteriorated, as the caliph, ruling from Baghdad, began losing much of his central authority over the realms his state once possessed. In the East with the Samanids of Iran and in the West with the Tulunids of Egypt, the caliphs had gradually lost their command over their many territories, which had ceased to belong to them in all but name.

There are many explanations for why this downfall began, but the most central of these owes itself to much earlier events, with the arrival of a new demographic that had been imported into the caliphate, the Turks. The Turks were a nomadic people. They had built empires in the Central Asian Steppe for centuries and had contended with the dynasties of China for even longer. For their renowned and highly valued fighting prowess, these warriors were initially brought in as slave soldiers by the caliphate, as early as the 9th century.

And upon their conversion to Islam and their upbringing in a system of military training, they were made to be the fiercest fighters in the Middle East, completely dominating the Abbasid military by the middle of the 800s. By then, most of the leadership positions, once held by the

Arabs, were given instead to the Turks, who took their place and almost entirely replaced them altogether. It would not be long before they quickly seized control of and effectively ruled the caliphate.

In 1055, after the Abbasid Caliph, Al-Qa'im, sought their help to restore his authority over the rival Buyid dynasty, the Turks, led by Tughril Bey, marched into Baghdad and seized control. Now ruling a territory that encompassed Iran and Iraq, Tughril Bey was then honored by the caliph. He was recognized for the first time with the title of *sultan*, an Arabic word meaning "authority." This was the rise of the Seljuk state. And thus, the Abbasids became little more than figureheads, powerless and disabled from actually governing the empire that bore their name.

In North Africa, the caliphate's westernmost provinces fell under the control of a new entity, one which openly challenged Baghdad for leadership over the Ummah. This was the Fatimid Caliphate, the Ismaili-Shia dynasty that rivaled, threatened, and opposed the Abbasids in the books of religion, the courts of power, and the fields of battle. After the conquest of Egypt by the Fatimids in 969, they and the Abbasids would remain locked in hostility, a conflict so divisive that it cut deeper the divide between the millions of Muslims.

And from their schools in Al-Qahira, the doctrine of the Fatimids professed their own interpretation of Islam, one where the imam, from the family of the Prophet Muhammad

ﷺ, held complete spiritual and divine authority over the faith. For years, this fire of infighting would burn, until the unity that marked the Islamic civilization became no more with the rise of the Fatimid-Ismaili entity.

For a whole century, from 930 to 1030, a caliph in Baghdad, another caliph in Cairo, and even a third caliph in Cordoba contested for the mantle of rulership over the Muslims. And ultimately, all three of them failed to strengthen the Ummah, primarily because of the infighting that they had entrenched themselves into. In the case of the Abbasids, it was primarily because they were weak and powerless that they were thrust into these years of peril. But there were also times where it was because a caliph held far too much power, that led to them actively endangering the Ummah itself.

In the case of the Fatimids, they very well could have been responsible for triggering one of the greatest calamities the Muslim world has seen. The casus belli, cited by the Crusaders, was the threat posed by the Seljuk Turks to Constantinople, the Christians of the Near East, and the Church of the Holy Sepulchre. But even before this, one of the earlier episodes that severely damaged Muslim-Christian relations originated with the Fatimids of Egypt.

Within the two split branches of Islam, Sunnism and Shiism, there is an offshoot sect of Shiism that still has a few followers even today. This is Ismaili Shiism. The Ismailis emerged in opposition to mainstream Twelver Shia Islam, asserting that the recognized successor to Imam Jafar As-Sadiq, his son, Musa Al-Kazim, was not the true imam. They instead pledged their allegiance to his other son, Ismail Ibn Jafar. And thus, the Ismailis split from mainstream Shiism and became an extreme sect. But what distinguished them was their divergence from Shia quietism. Twelvers believed in the divinity of their line of imams, insisting that political ambitions, such as a caliphate, were lesser, worldly pursuits and thus beneath the imamate.

Ismailism, as it gained traction in North Africa, at the fringe edges of the Abbasid realm, was beginning to put forth its vision of a Shia caliphate. This finally materialized with the birth of the Fatimid Caliphate and its first leader, Abdallah Al-Mahdi Billah, when he was declared both imam and caliph. From their first capital, Mahdiyya, in modern day Tunisia, the Fatimids enlisted and secured the support of local Berber tribes. As their army grew, they expanded across North Africa, briefly into Sicily, and then eventually upon Egypt. In 969, Fustat was conquered. And it was here that the rival metropolis to Baghdad was built, serving as the new capital of this Shia caliphate, the city of Cairo, *Al-Qahira* in Arabic.

But the destabilization of the Ummah, which occurred at the hands of the Fatimids, can be seen in the reign of the man, known as "the Mad Caliph," Abu Ali Al-Mansur, Al-Hakim bi-Amr Allah. Under his reign, the caliphate had been in control of additional territories in the Muslim world, including Jerusalem, Mecca, and Medina. Most of the subjects of these lands were still Sunni Muslim, even within Egypt itself. And so when the Fatimids propagated their Ismaili doctrine, the populace of their caliphate found their creed so foreign that they quickly became a despised group for their deviance.

The Ismailis incorporated, into their acts of worship, phrases of condemnation that cursed many of the Sahaba, which nearly all Muslims, except for this sect, held great love for. And especially in Jerusalem, where the legacy of the Sahaba was so engrained, such as with the memory of the second caliph, Omar Ibn Khattab (رضي الله عنه), who conquered Jerusalem, the Fatimids tried to reorient the reverence of the Muslims towards their creed instead, away from these revered men of the past.

And in the year 996, Al-Hakim bi-Amr Allah, when he ascended to the throne as a child, at the age of 14, he began to further alienate the Muslims from the legitimacy of his rule. Strangely, he began attributing to himself characteristics of divine nature, much to the discomfort of the people. And this continued throughout his reign, often intensifying and seeping its way into the lives of his subjects, such as with praises of his name during the call to prayer from the mosques, in the Friday sermons, or even in the middle of the prayers themselves. Finally, perhaps as the epitome of his departure from mainstream Islam, he banned Hajj, the pilgrimage to Mecca, believing that the Kaaba drew too much popularity away from him and his special creed.

In 1009, his radical deviance then grew to become painfully harmful to the Christians, living under his rule. In that year, whilst in the midst of a dispute with the Byzantine Romans, he ordered the desecration of the Church of the Holy Sepulchre in Jerusalem, breaking the tradition of respect that was first established by Omar Ibn Khattab (رضي الله عنه). Such a crime, which had been unprecedented and actually forbidden in the history of the Muslims, disturbed not just Constantinople, but also sent shockwaves into the heart of Europe. In the eyes of the Pope, Jerusalem had been violated by disbelievers.

Finally, in 1021, after spending the years of his reign, desecrating holy sites, alienating his people, infuriating both the Christian and Muslim worlds, truly behaving as a "mad caliph," he disappears. One evening, he walks outside his capital, ventures beyond the edges of the city, and is never seen again. Some followers believe that this was his final act of divinity, as this was his moment of occultation, for he was the true hidden imam, who would return to save mankind. While fringe movements deify him as a saint, most of his subjects see him closer to who he actually was, an erratic, perhaps mentally ill monarch. From both polar angles, he was nonetheless a fascinatingly strange human being to say the least.

Whatever the reason for his disappearance, because of him and the madness of his rule, Christian-Muslim relations would never be the same. The damage that he inflicted on the international stage was immensely detrimental to the stability of the region and the image of the Muslims. While the Church of the Holy Sepulchre would be rebuilt in 1039 and his successors did reverse many of his policies, his actions had already angered the whole of Christendom. The damage had been done.

Across the Mediterranean, in Western Europe, while the idea of freeing God's land, from such a despised religion, existed in the imagination of many at the time, Europe was beset with its own problems at home. The 11th century was an era of great famine, plague, and infighting between the houses of the feudal realms. While the Islamic World in the East advanced in the fields of science, Europe languished in the midst of its economic impoverishment. And this was compounded with political instability.

As was the reality for many communities, when the feudal lord of one town ran his estate and appointed his favorite son as his deputy, the rest of the brothers looked to find their own ways of wealth and power. And they found it often in robbery and looting against other feudal towns, a trend that would only escalate as the princes and kings of the continent waged war against one another and incentivized their knights to plunder for their own gain. While the feudal lords engaged in such a destructive cycle of conflict with each other, the single true authority that could bind the continent together rested in the hands of the Papacy.

At a time when Europe's population was decreasing, poverty and famine was increasing, and corruption was spreading across the feudal lands, the wealth and influence possessed by the Catholic Church far exceeded those of Europe's monarchs. And in the face of the widespread turmoil and unrest that gripped Europe in the 1000s, many popes over the years understood that such desire, for war and wealth amongst the warrior and noble classes, needed to be redirected outside of Europe, towards lands which the Papacy held ambitions for.

This new land was indeed the Holy Land. Jerusalem rested at its center. With the threat of the Muslims inching far too close to Constantinople, to the very gates of Europe, in the form of the Seljuk Turks' victories at Manzikert in 1071, the capture of Nicaea in 1081, and the rapid conquest of most of Anatolia in that small period of time, the Papacy found an even more pressing justification to declare war against Islam.

On November 27th, 1095, as the council of feudal lords was assembled in the town of Clermont, in France, Pope Urban II would give arguably the most impactful speech of the Middle Ages, thus declaring the future between Islam and Christendom, between East and West, for the next 600 years. Its impact would ripple across time, from the Crusades in the Levant to the Reconquista in Spain, and even much later in the language used by the United States in its justification for invading Iraq. He announced the formation of the First Crusade, a holy war in the name of religion, to reconquer Jerusalem and the Holy Land from the Muslims. He would point to the neglect of the Church of the Holy Sepulchre, under the Muslims, and the threat posed to the Eastern Christians, calling for Europe's armies to intervene.

According to Robert the Monk, one of the chroniclers from the time, the Pope was written to have said on that day in Clermont:

"For, as most of you have heard, the Saracens have attacked them and have conquered the territory of Romania [Byzantium].... They destroy the churches of God or use them for their own rites. They are **a race alien to God**, a generation that has not directed its heart and whose spirit is not faithful to God."

In dehumanizing the Muslims or "Saracens," as the Crusaders called them, degrading them, as lesser than human, in the eyes of the people, the Pope was giving license to kill, steal, and desecrate. Within such incendiary language, the Pope may have orated one of the earliest and most consequential pieces of propaganda in European history, forever changing the course of history for the West and the Middle East. And he would promise more.

He called on any and all men to join the armies of the Crusade, many of whom were murderers or thieves. Criminals would be exonerated. All of their debts would be forgiven. And if they killed a Saracen, it would not be murder, but instead their right of passage to heaven. They would be forgiven of all their sins and their place in the afterlife would be guaranteed. This conflict was now a religious war, a righteous cause to justify an enterprise that was really driven by an economic opportunity to enrich Europe's nobility and their knights.

The entire Crusader venture was composed not only of Europe's nobles, clergy, and knights, but also its merchants. The Italian republics of Venice, Genoa, and Pisa were just as instrumental on the sea lanes, to the establishment of the Crusader states in the Levant, as the armies were on the battlefields. The Genoese dispatched a fleet, in 1097, to support the Crusaders in besieging Antioch, sending supplies and transport vessels. Genoa also won various trading privileges in cities like Latakia and Jaffa, setting up commercial colonies, the first of their kind, long before the trading colonies or economic zones of Portugal, Britain, or the US emerged on the world map. Pisa and Venice also gained lucrative opportunities in these ventures. For their naval support, both had gained trading rights and even city quarters within Jerusalem and Acre, as early as 1099.

Upon conquering Jerusalem and completing the mission of their campaign, the land armies of the First Crusade proceeded to enact one of the most infamous episodes of human crime. The infamous massacre of the First Crusade left behind enough blood to wet the streets of Jerusalem in pools of red. Eyewitnesses, some even from among the Crusade, such as Raymond of Aguilers, recount that the fall of Jerusalem produced some of the most gruesome atrocities of the time. The city was littered with piles of heads, arms, hands, and feet. Corpses lay in the streets.

Those who were fortunate enough to survive, fled to the hills east of the city. They saw their ruined home from afar with the smoke rising like the signature of the enemy's actions. This new age of European warfare and colonial enterprise would forever be known by the world, half admiringly and half resentfully, as *the Crusades*. It was a venture that pillaged the Muslim world under a religious cause. The heinous crime, that marked the opening chapter of this new era, would not go unforgiven, as it would usher in decades of conflict between the Muslims and the Crusaders, lasting for almost 200 years and beyond.

Chapter 4
The Calling

Bab Zuweila, Cairo, Egypt

There is a unique hadith by the Prophet Muhammad ﷺ, wherein he was chronicled to have told his companions:

"I asked my Lord for three things. I asked Him that my Ummah not be destroyed by drought. He granted that. I asked Him that they should not be defeated by an external enemy. He granted me that. And then I asked Him that it be not divided by internal discord. However, this one was withheld."

- Prophet Muhammad ﷺ [Tirmidhi 2175]

The divisions that, even now, continue to afflict the Muslim world, are not merely political struggles of a few corrupt men. In the Islamic paradigm, as foretold by the Prophet ﷺ, division is a test from God and a responsibility upon the Muslims to overcome themselves. 64 years after the First Crusade, in 1163, a diplomatic mission from Cairo traveled to Damascus. Upon arriving at the city's gates, the Egyptian delegation was given entry into the city. The man at the head of this mission was the deposed Vizier Shawar Al-Saadi of the Fatimid Caliphate.

Following the arrival of the Crusades, the Fatimids attempted to regain some of their holdings in Palestine, but their wars against the newly established Kingdom of Jerusalem failed to reassert control over their former lands. Thus, the power of the Fatimids waned, and their empire was reduced only to the Egyptian heartland. And so, they too entered a miserable decline, a sickness common amongst the rivaling states of the Middle East.

Shawar Al-Saadi himself was not Shia but Sunni. His service towards the Fatimid Caliphate was not out of religious or ideological alignment, but rather out of political opportunism. As the highest minister in Fatimid Egypt, Shawar had once enjoyed the influence, authority, and wealth that came with one of the most significant seats of power in the world. And he was intent on regaining that power. In 1163, the decline of the Fatimids had put them on the brink of total collapse. The Fatimid state had deteriorated so far that its conquest at the hands of the Crusaders seemed almost inevitable.

In Syria, Shawar and his entourage made their way to the sultan's estate. Despite no longer possessing any existing title or authority, Shawar traveled on behalf of the powerless Fatimid Caliph, Al-Adid. Inside, the palace guard notified the sultan and his most esteemed general, Asadeddin Shirkuh, of the arrival of their guest. The sultan granted permission, allowing Shawar to enter and come forth before his presence.

Shawar had come, seeking an audience with the Zengid leader, delivering him news of the deteriorating situation in Egypt. The King of Jerusalem, Amalric I, had fortified the city of Askalan, next to Gaza. From this base, Crusader incursions into Egypt were growing each year. The Fatimids were in part disabled from leading a coordinated defense of their dominion because of the rule of a usurper from Yemen, Dirgham, whose instability greatly depleted the capabilities of the Fatimid state. Shawar then proceeded to request military support from Nureddin, to secure the borders of Egypt from the Crusaders, to overthrow Dirgham, and to reinstate himself as Vizier of Egypt. Thus, he would serve as a dependable ally to Syria.

Nureddin initially hesitated to make any promises. He had held ambitions of his own to conquer Egypt and unite it together with Syria, constructing a vast empire that would effectively surround and overwhelm the Crusader states. For the first few weeks of Shawar's visit to Damascus, Nureddin would delay in giving him his answer. Finally, after Crusader incursions intensified in those weeks, Nureddin would announce his support for Shawar Al-Saadi, agreeing to send forth an army into Egypt.

For the Zengid sultan, preventing Egypt from falling at the hands of the Crusaders was now at the forefront of his geopolitical agenda. Egypt was a country of immense resources and naturally had the ability to act as a major player in the region. Its fertile land made it one of, if not, the most productive agricultural region in the world. Egypt was a major grain producer of wheat and barley. Rice, especially from the green, wet fields of the Nile Delta, was cultivated to sustain millions. This made Egypt by far the largest supplier of grain in the eastern Mediterranean. Lentils and beans were also grown. Lucrative crops like sugarcane were also part of the agricultural economy, as well as cotton in the textile sector. And perhaps most crucially, Egyptian farmland around the Nile River was so vast that the country was able to also sustain livestock like cattle, sheep, goats, chicken, and ducks, placing Egypt far ahead of the rest of the region in terms of raising and slaughtering farm animals. And while Syria hosted a population of approximately 2 to 3 million people, Egypt's population constituted a figure estimated between 5 to 7 million.

Thus, for Sultan Nureddin Zengi, Egypt would be the most crucial step of his entire career. Egypt, with all the strength of its economy and population, had the potential to drive forward the vision of Muslim revivalism. Without Egypt united with Syria, the path to reconquering Palestine from the Crusaders would have been a far more arduous, perhaps even an impossible endeavor. For Nureddin, Jerusalem was the endgame.

For the long awaited day that it would be retaken, Nureddin had his artisans build a minbar, a wooden pulpit, to be installed in Al-Aqsa when it would be freed at last. The attention to detail in this masterpiece of carpentry demonstrated impressive craftsmanship with ebony and ivory, along with ornate Kufic engravings and floral patterns. Such dedication by the designers of the minbar illustrated just how deep Jerusalem was in the imagination of the Muslims. Despite the political realities that they were beset with, they nonetheless planned meticulously for that day. And in 1163, Nureddin Zengi understood that the path towards that endgame was through Egypt.

1930 Photo of the Minbar of Nureddin Zengi in Al-Aqsa, Jerusalem, Palestine

The commander that Nureddin appointed to lead the campaign was the brother of Najmeddin. He was a Kurdish warrior and Zengid military commander, Asadeddin Shirkuh, whose title, *Lion of the Faith*, was complemented by his birth name, which literally means "mountain lion." This lion of the Kurds fought for the Zengids in many campaigns, even losing an eye in battle, forcing him to dawn a patch over his injury, giving him a striking appearance. By now, the two Kurdish brothers had integrated themselves closely within the inner circle of Nureddin, becoming two of his most valued advisers.

Salahuddin too had risen through the ranks, and Nureddin had been watching him with great interest, as his teacher. And so when it was announced that the Zengid state would support Shawar with an army, Nureddin placed his confidence behind the family of Ayyub to execute his policy of securing Egypt. However, when Shirkuh asked Salahuddin to join the war to reclaim Egypt, he was reluctant. At that time, Salahuddin simply wanted to live out a career as a scholar, seeing the ulema with high regard.

Over time, however, Salahuddin's perspective began to shift. As he witnessed the Crusaders' cruelty, their occupation of Jerusalem, and the possibility that they could seize Egypt, a deep desire to defeat them and reclaim Al-Aqsa grew within him. And so together, Shirkuh and his nephew embarked upon Egypt. Setting out from Damascus, Shirkuh would lead his army south before crossing into the Sinai Peninsula, a journey which would take approximately three weeks.

Within the ranks of soldiers that followed him, there were Kurds, Turks, as well as Arabs. Fighting beside Shirkuh were his two most trusted bodyguards, Saifeddin Yazkoj and Arslan Bogha, Mamluks of Turkic backgrounds. In addition to soldiers, Shirkuh also brought with him men of knowledge. Isa Al-Hakkari was a Kurdish doctor, scholar, and imam from

Aleppo. He too had joined the ranks of Shirkuh's army and served as its imam.

By the time they were past Shobak, in Jordan, they had already completed half of the march. And soon, the terrain turned to rough sand and the weather grew ferociously hot in the middle hours of the day. Within days, the Zengid army had arrived in Egypt. It emerged from the Sinai desert and was welcomed by the supporters of Shawar Al-Saadi. Shirkuh immediately sent his men to execute the orders of their sultan. Shirkuh's Turkic cavalry traveled on the roads, occupying towns and taking over several forts and strategic houses. These horsemen, the Ghulams and Mamluks, ravaged Dirgham's lines of communication and dismembered his apparatus with ease. Within days, Shirkuh and his nephew were mounted on their horses, atop a hill, overlooking the eastern Nile plateau, as it was being flooded by their rapidly advancing army.

When they reached Cairo, the defenders of the walls surrendered. Asadeddin Shirkuh stepped foot inside the city, followed by his army of Turkic and Kurdish warriors. He and his men had secured a quick and decisive victory for their sultan. As for the usurper himself, Dirgham had been killed by a mob of disgruntled Egyptian civilians. Shirkuh stood his ground, and it paid off with the feat of securing Al-Qahira, the capital of Egypt, for his country's new ally, Shawar Al-Saadi. He would be immediately appointed to his old office, as Vizier of Fatimid Egypt.

Chapter 5
A Knife's Edge

Bab Al-Futuh, Cairo, Egypt

The operation in securing Cairo ended in a victory for the Zengids, in the year 1164. Having seized full control of the capital, Shirkuh had completed the mission assigned to him by his master. And it was from the city walls that overlooked the eastern plateau, did he witness the work that he had achieved, the capture of Egypt.

However, Shirkuh and his men would not depart from Egypt just yet. The general had taken his men and encamped at the city of Bilbeis. There they would remain for several months, occupying the town and the borders of the country, so as to protect the struggling Fatimid state from renewed Crusader incursions into Egypt. This was not what Shawar Al-Saadi had intended. He, along with many in the Fatimid government, were not given a sense of security with the sight of a Sunni Turkic army, resting within the borders of their state. Instead, Shawar was growing anxious, vexed by Shirkuh in particular. The general was alleged to have boasted to his men, during times of raising the morale of the army, that he would one day make himself "the master of Masr."

Such ambitions of ruling Egypt gave Shawar reason to fear Shirkuh. Immediately, he looked for alternative allies. And he found them in the Crusaders. Opening a channel of communication between himself and King Amalric I of Jerusalem, Shawar forged, in secret, a Fatimid-Crusader alliance against the Zengid army of Asadeddin Shirkuh. That year, in 1164, as tensions continued to rise between Shawar Al-Saadi and Shirkuh, the Zengids came under attack at Bilbeis. The Crusaders laid siege to the city. Surrounded, betrayed, and in foreign land, the men of Shirkuh attempted to resist and managed to hold out for days.

Upon receiving news of this disturbing and flagrant act of betrayal, Nureddin Zengi was quick to act. In a move to save his general, and taking the advice of his younger brother, Kotbeddin Zengi, Nureddin moved to attack the County of Tripoli, one of the Crusader states, in present day Lebanon. Within the army of Amalric I, many of the knights and nobles that traveled with the king into Egypt were from Tripoli. Thus, when news arrived of a Muslim attack on his most crucial ally, Amalric was pressured to relinquish the Egyptian campaign and withdraw. Once the Crusaders had ceased to besiege Bilbeis and returned back across the border, Shirkuh seized the opportunity to withdraw as well.

And so the Zengid army departed from Bilbeis, fleeing back to Syria, as a bleeding army. Their rivalry with the Crusaders finally erupted into open war, and the Fatimid Vizier, Shawar Al-Saadi, whom they had helped reinstate only the year prior, had betrayed them. Still, battered and wounded, they would live to fight another day. Then, before they crossed into Sinai, Salahuddin turned back to see the majestic land that was Egypt one last time, as if he would never return to witness the ancient Nile again. Perhaps, as he traveled with the army on the road back to Syria, did he dwell on the loss, which he and his men had suffered. Their efforts, which were spent in the struggle to reunite the Ummah, had been in vain, one would think.

However, Salahuddin was not educated to see the world through a defeatist mentality. His vision, as that of his leaders and teachers, was one that looked beyond the present challenges at hand. One defeat would not derail their movement of revival. And soon, he and his uncle would return to Egypt once more.

Chapter 6
Masters

Giza, Egypt

The road back to Damascus was long and grueling, for along the way, the fast winds blew sand into the faces and eyes of the traveling soldiers. The land became dryer and more unforgiving with less food to forge on and scarcer water to survive on. So, when the Zengid army finally reached the edge of Damascus, the guards of the city walls witnessed many within the morale-depleted army collapse to the ground. Their expedition had finally ended.

Shirkuh would return to his leader, Nureddin, and report to him the complete summary of the events that transpired in Egypt. Nureddin was furious. From backing Shawar as his supporter to suffering from betrayal at his hand, Nureddin understood that the score needed to be settled. But the sultan would be patient. For the next three years, Nureddin and Shirkuh would wait, attentively watching the situation unfold from the safety of their borders in Syria.

During this time, Salahuddin also waited. One would imagine how he must have anticipated the next expedition into Egypt. The aspirations, held by his uncle, were shared by him also. Listening to his uncle speak of one day becoming the "master of Masr," was a vision that Salahuddin long awaited for as well. For him and within his worldview, every step taken towards the revival of the Muslims was a step closer to liberating Al-Aqsa, in Jerusalem. One of the stories of Salahuddin's childhood speaks of him playing with a group of boys. Then his father, Najmeddin, came to take him.

He snatched him by his arm and scolded him, saying, " I did not marry your mother, so you could play with other children but to liberate Al-Aqsa."

He then threw him to the ground, taking out his frustration and anger upon the boy. But, according to his biography by Bahaddin Ibn Shaddad, in this scene, the boy did not break. His youthful visage emitted only the look of control and maturity. His father asked him, "Did it not hurt?" "Yes," he answered. Then why did you not cry?" Najmeddin asked. "It is not fitting for the conqueror of Al-Aqsa to cry," he told him. Not even a soldier, let alone a teenager, Salahuddin's dream of liberating Al-Aqsa was very much part of his identity from the very beginning. And in 1167, Salahuddin would receive a second chance to advance towards the fulfillment of this dream, shared by every Muslim revivalist. In that year, as Shawar's delicate relationship with the Kingdom of Jerusalem was once again put under heavy strain by renewed Crusader incursions into Egypt, Nureddin seized at this opportunity.

The sultan once again sent his general, Asadeddin Shirkuh, and his young, 30-year old lieutenant, Salahuddin to the battlefield once more. The two returned to Egypt with their army of 10,000, but found themselves standing before the hostility of both the Crusaders and the Fatimids. In the first days of this second campaign into the country, Shirkuh, having learned his lesson from Bilbeis, understood that he needed to avoid direct confrontation with both armies. He would fight them separately and on his own terms.

The day was March 18th, 1167. Asadeddin Shirkuh, his nephew, and his army stood outside the vicinity of Cairo. On his orders, the Zengid army, upon spotting the Crusaders, raced southwest. Seeking to inflict a decisive defeat upon their opponents, the Crusaders elected to pursue them south of Giza, past the Great Pyramids, at a spot known as Al-Babein. When the Zengids halted their feigned retreat and turned around to face their enemy, they saw the true size of their opponent's force.

The Muslims had close to 10,000, while their adversary numbered at least 17,000. With an uphill battle before him, Shirkuh conjured a strategy that would effectively disable the Crusaders of their numerical advantage. Salahuddin was given an eyepatch by his uncle, as part of the plan to deceive the enemy army into assuming that he was Shirkuh, the leader of the army. Shirkuh then galloped away with his cavalry and Mamluks. Once he was gone, Salahuddin was left to assume command of his army group.

When the Crusaders finally arrived, he knew precisely what he would do next. He took his battalion and proceeded to flee a second time, leading them deeper and deeper into the desert. Further away, the approaching Crusaders found themselves bewildered in the middle of the open desert of the Giza Plateau. Over confident in their capabilities, the Crusaders were fooled into continuing their advance into the desolate landscape, far past the Great Pyramids. The further the Muslims kept them on the march, the more spread out their lines became. And it was not long before they began to suffer from fatigue and exhaustion under the merciless sun.

At that moment, Shirkuh finally emerged from the desert and intervened to pick them off. His cavalry moved in and out of the area, harassing their opponents, and then returning to the safety of the dunes. They met minimal resistance, even from the Crusader cavalry, whose horses struggled to move in the deep sand.

With the sun showing no mercy and the desert offering no help to the dangerously scattered army, the Crusaders looked up the hill that sat before them, only to be met by the full force of their adversary. The Muslims, under Salahuddin, had rushed down the slope to finish them. What had once started out as small skirmishes, by Shirkuh's light cavalry, turned into a complete and total assault by both groups upon their helpless enemy. In the chaos, the soldiers looked for their king, desperate for orders to change their doomed fate. But King Amalric, having lost control of the situation, fled the battle and retreated back to the borders of his kingdom. By the day's end, the Crusaders littered the ground as corpses. The soldiers of Salahuddin and Shirkuh stood proudly above them, celebrating their victory.

In the following year, in 1168, after leaving Salahuddin in Egypt behind to supervise the army, Shirkuh returned again, as part of a third campaign into the country. This time, he both defeated the Crusaders of Amalric and moved to occupy Cairo. The triumph of the Zengids rang loud through the streets of Al-Qahira when Shirkuh set foot into the city. With the approval of the Fatimid caliph, Asadeddin Shirkuh proclaimed himself as the new vizier. He was now the master of Masr, and his first act was to execute Shawar for his treachery.

With Fatimid support for him all but gone, the former ruler scrambled to escape from the Fatimid palace complex. It was there that he was trapped and placed under arrest. Shirkuh had sent his right hand, Salahuddin, to personally apprehend him. On his orders, the disgraced vizier was then put to the sword, executed for his treachery in collaborating with the Crusaders. With Shawar dead and nothing standing in his way, Shirkuh made a visit to the Fatimid palace and signed a new treaty with the Caliph Al-Adid, effectively confirming his authority as the vizier. Nureddin received the message from Cairo, detailing the success of his general and pleasing his ears upon learning of the victory of his men.

However, the administration of Asadeddin Shirkuh would not last long. One evening, after a dinner feast at his new estate in Cairo, Shirkuh was burdened with severe quinsy in the throat. The pain he suffered brought him to the floor, stirring panic among his companions, particularly his nephew, who immediately rushed to his aid. Doctor Isa Al-Hakkari was summoned to help treat him, but it was to no avail. On the 23rd of March, 1169, just two months into his administration, Shirkuh died and was buried outside the city. Salahuddin stood before his grave, mourning for his general, his uncle, his teacher. While he contemplated what he would do without him, the death of Egypt's vizier left a void in need of filling.

At the palace assembly, Shirkuh's successor was at the center of the discourse. One of the chief jurists was Qadi Al-Fadil, a Palestinian lawyer, scholar, and judge from the city of Askalan, who had been trained under the Fatimid administration. He emphasized to the council the need to put personal differences aside, to elect a capable successor, who would serve for the betterment and reconstruction of the country.

Many voiced their minds in agreement with his statement. However, there were others who feared such change at the hands of the Zengid Turks. They protested and fierce arguments ensued. After the debate's uproar subsided, a messenger arrived from Damascus. Nureddin had intervened in their session, personally recommending that Salahuddin be made vizier.

All eyes then turned to the 30-year-old commander. To the likes of Qadi Al-Fadil, he was a well-educated man and an experienced military leader. Others, more hardline members of the Fatimid court, gave their support out of calculation that, because of his age and perhaps also his lack of political experience, they could control him.

By the end of the session, nearly every member had endorsed Salahuddin, and he won by a majority of the vote. And with the final seal of approval by the caliph, Salahuddin was confirmed as Vizier of Fatimid Egypt. When the assembly concluded and all were dismissed, Salahuddin retreated to the balcony with his Mamluks, his supporters, and Qadi Al-Fadil.

For the next five years, Salahuddin, alongside this new circle of support, would assume authority over Egypt, governing the country with resolve and a sense of direction. He would oversee the reconstruction of cities, the revitalization of trade routes, and the growth of economic wealth. And the army, most importantly, would be restored with renewed strength, bolstered by the arrival of Mamluks from Syria. With each passing year, Salahuddin's name would spread, making him known as a symbol of Islamic justice and revival. And his journey had only begun.

Part II
The Sultan
(1169 - 1177)

Statue of Salahuddin
Baghdad, Iraq

Murad 69

Chapter 7
By Will of the Pen

Dirham of Salahuddin (1182 - 1183)

"Let there be a group among you who calls others to goodness, encourages what is good, and forbids what is evil. It is they who will be successful."

وَلْتَكُن مِّنكُمْ أُمَّةٌ يَدْعُونَ إِلَى ٱلْخَيْرِ وَيَأْمُرُونَ بِٱلْمَعْرُوفِ وَيَنْهَوْنَ عَنِ ٱلْمُنكَرِ ۚ وَأُو۟لَـٰٓئِكَ هُمُ ٱلْمُفْلِحُونَ

- Surah Al-Imran of the Quran (3:104)

    Upon becoming the Vizier of Egypt, effectively a 12th-century prime minister, Salahuddin gave his allegiance, not to the Abbasid caliph in Baghdad, but instead to the Ismaili Caliph, Al-Adid. And so at the start of his political career,

Salahuddin was, at least in name, a Fatimid statesman. His religious convictions, as a Sunni Muslim, did not waver, but, as he served the Fatimid Caliphate, he remained collected and patient, careful not to create enemies.

For the first year of his administration, Salahuddin dedicated his attention to the reconstruction of Egypt's infrastructure and economy. He commissioned hospitals and universities. He poured resources into various public works, such as roads, bridges, and city defense fortifications. He also directed projects that oversaw the manufacture of vessels and ships, which would be used for trade, especially in the Red Sea and Indian Ocean. With the country's resources, manpower, and time, Salahuddin was poised to return Egypt to its place, as a leading player in the Muslim world.

However, there would come opposition to his progress. Salahuddin was proactive in organizing a security service for his administration, gathering intelligence on potential threats to the state. Just a few months into his time in office as vizier, his spies reported to him and uncovered a plot by various Fatimid conspirators to overthrow his administration and assassinate him. Ever distrustful of a Sunni vizier, leading their state, the Fatimids planned to destabilize and topple his rule.

Salahuddin, acting with a sense of urgency and swift determination, would not allow the threat to permeate within his rule, and so he would have his bodyguards arrest the suspected ringleader and execute him in a public square before Cairo's populace. But instead of sending a warning, this only triggered the rest of the collaborators to take action. Across Egypt, in almost every city, rebels took the streets and fighting ensued between the forces of the conspirators and Salahuddin's soldiers.

The uprising lasted 6 months before finally Salahuddin crushed the opposition with his security forces. No amnesty or forgiveness was granted to any of the dissenting conspirators. Through his resolute actions, Salahuddin prevailed in restoring the image of his rule, projecting stability and sending a warning to any potential challengers that he was in Egypt to stay. No plot could overthrow him, so long as he had the ears to detect it and the men to dismember it.

Where there was suspicion, Salahuddin replaced it with loyalty, installing family members and close advisors, whom he could trust. Qadi Al-Fadil, the Palestinian judge and scholar of the Fatimid court, had been one of Salahuddin's closest allies and dearest companions. His role within his administration would only elevate, as he proved himself as a trustworthy and reputable official. Al-Adil, Salahuddin's younger brother, arrived, as did his second brother, Turanshah. Both would be installed as key members of his government.

With his position strengthened after the rebellion, Salahuddin turned to reorient the Egyptian nation back to the fold of Sunni Islam. In the first year of his reign, he was patient with the Ismaili practices that permeated through Egyptian life. But now, with the advice of Qadi Al-Fadil, he moved to slowly and carefully remove these elements. The Shia adhan, the call to prayer, was known to have differed from that of the Sunni tradition. Salahuddin mandated that it follow the Sunni tradition and call the people back to the way of the Sunnah. Shia festivals like Ghadir Khumm and Ashura, which were also prominent under the Fatimids, gradually were restricted, until Salahuddin banned them altogether.

And the universities, such as Al-Azhar, which propagated the views of the Ismaili creed in conflict with the rest of the Muslim world, were also redirected by the new administration. Salahuddin would invite and appoint Sunni scholars, build new madrasas, and instruct all of them to adhere to a Sunni curriculum.

None of these changes could have been achieved if it were not for Salahuddin's chief jurist on Islamicate affairs, Qadi Al-Fadil. The two men, who were likely around the same age, Qadi Al-Fadil, born in 1135, and Salahuddin in 1137, developed a close connection and realized early on that they belonged to the same ideals of Muslim revivalism. With Salahuddin's vision of reintroducing Egypt back to Sunni Islam and Qadi Al-Fadil's familiarity and experience in the legal administration of the country, the two succeeded in dismantling the Fatimid regime and replacing it with an administration, adherent to the Sunnah.

Speaking of the value he attached to his minister, Salahuddin would remark, "I took Egypt not by force of arms but by the pen of Qadi Al-Fadil."

Finally, with the death of the last Fatimid Caliph, Al-Adid, Salahuddin would instruct all the Friday sermons, in the mosques, to be read out in his name. Every minted dinar, dirham, and coin would bear his name, as the ruler of the land. Political recognition would be given to him, not a Fatimid caliph. He would also pledge his allegiance to the Abbasid caliph in Baghdad, thus completing the return of Egypt's identity back to Sunnism. And to cement his authority further, Salahuddin would abandon the title of vizier altogether and declare himself the sultan. He was now the founder of the Ayyubid dynasty, and Egypt was his sultanate.

Chapter 8
David's Descendants

Dinar of Salahuddin (1184)

"They are not all alike. Among the People of the Book is a group that is upright. They recite the verses of Allah during the hours of the night, prostrating [in prayer]. They believe in Allah and the Last Day, and they enjoin what is right and forbid what is wrong and hasten to good deeds. And those are among the righteous."

لَيْسُوا سَوَاءً مِّنْ أَهْلِ ٱلْكِتَٰبِ أُمَّةٌ قَآئِمَةٌ يَتْلُونَ ءَايَٰتِ ٱللَّهِ ءَانَآءَ ٱلَّيْلِ وَهُمْ يَسْجُدُونَ
يُؤْمِنُونَ بِٱللَّهِ وَٱلْيَوْمِ ٱلْءَاخِرِ وَيَأْمُرُونَ بِٱلْمَعْرُوفِ وَيَنْهَوْنَ عَنِ ٱلْمُنكَرِ وَيُسَٰرِعُونَ فِى ٱلْخَيْرَٰتِ وَأُوْلَٰٓئِكَ مِنَ ٱلصَّٰلِحِينَ

- Surah Al-Imran (3:113-114)

The relationship that Salahuddin and many of his contemporaries had with the Jewish community, whom the Quran refers to as *Ahl Al-Kitab*, "People of the Book," was shaped by experiences that trace back to the early days of the Muslim faith. Before the birth of Islam, Jews had lived for centuries in the Arabian Peninsula, existing alongside the ancient Arab tribes of the region. Within the lifetime of the Prophet Muhammad ﷺ, there were several established Jewish communities across Arabia, including Yathrib, the town that would become Medina. The Jews coexisted alongside Christians, pagans, and Zoroastrians. There were also unique groups within this demographic, such as the Ebionites, a group synthesized from Judaism and Christianity, who recognized Jesus (عليه السلام) as the Messiah, but elected to follow Jewish law, diverting from the Chrsitian tradition of Paul.

When the Prophet Muhammad ﷺ made the migration to Medina, for the first time, his followers would be exposed to interactions with the Jews, unlike in Mecca, where such diversity did not exist. Setting a precedent for his successors, the Prophet ﷺ administered, not just as a tolerant ruler, but as a mediator between the various groups in Medina. The Constitution of Medina made Jews and other believers citizens of equanimous status, recognizing them as individual communities within their own right, who deserved to be granted respect, protection, and freedom under Muslim rule.

There were, however, battles, which the early Muslims fought against some of the dissenting Jewish tribes of Arabia, like those against Banu Qurayza or the Battle of Khaybar. Tribes like Banu Nadir, Banu Qurayza, and Banu Qaynuqa all were involved in conflicts with the young Muslim state of Medina. Some cooperated with Quraysh against the Prophet ﷺ, involving themselves in attempts to attack his followers and undermine his rule in Medina. However, these emerged out of the geopolitical tensions of the time, rather than a clash of identity, racism, or antisemitism.

From a place of theology, the Quran sees the Psalms and Torah of the Hebrew Bible as holy scripture, revealed by God, that was altered over time. This view is also held for the Gospels of the New Testament. In fact, throughout the Quran, there are many chapters dedicated to the prophets that came before, many of them are revered in the Jewish scripture as well. And within these chapters, the followers of these prophets, the Jews themselves, are mentioned, giving the Jews, as a people, a place of recognition, legitimacy, and respect within the Islamic worldview.

When the Islamic Caliphate began its conquests in the Middle East and North Africa, few of its efforts were directed towards conversion. In fact, when Caliph Omar Ibn Khattab (رضي الله عنه) conquered Jerusalem, it was he who allowed the resettlement of Jews within the city, for it was the Christian

Romans, who deported them during the Byzantine-Persian wars. Omar's example thus set a precedent of tolerance, allowing the flourishing of Jewish communities across the Muslim world in the coming centuries, in Spain, Egypt, Syria, and Iraq.

Many Jews excelled through the opportunities of Muslim rule. For instance, the Abbasids entrusted the finances of their capital, Baghdad, to Jewish bankers. Jews were also given critical administrative positions in certain aspects of maritime trade and commerce. Siraf, one of the major port cities in the Gulf, even had a Jewish governor in the 10th century. Moreover, Jews played an invaluable role in the Golden Age of knowledge and academic research, for they were among those who helped translate many ancient texts to be preserved in the colleges in Baghdad, Cairo, and Cordoba. Up until 1948 with the creation of the State of Israel, one third of Baghdad's population was in fact Jewish.

By the end of the 900s, Cordoba, in particular, became one of the finest cities for Jews to succeed, likely more than anywhere else in the world. In sharp contrast to the antisemitism of Christian Europe, whose routine persecution of Ashkenazi Jews would persist for centuries to come, in Muslim Spain, the Sephardic Jews flourished under their local Andalusian rabbis, who represented their community under Islamic rule. Many Sephardic Jews would rise to positions of political significance, like, for instance, Samuel Ibn Naghrillah, a merchant and politician, who was appointed as the prime minister of Granada, a rare event that demonstrates the level of appreciation that Muslims had for the talented and skilled individuals of the society, regardless of their religious or ethnic background. Men like Samuel, with their elevated status in society, would use their wealth to fund the development of various Jewish communities across the Mediterranean.

During the time of Sultan Salahuddin, one of the most famous Jewish leaders was Musa Ibn Maymun, known in the West as *Moses Maimonides*. Born in Cordoba in 1135, Musa was trained to be a rabbinical judge, giving him a strong mastery of Halakha, Jewish law. But he was also highly educated in Greek philosophy and medicine. In the midst of his career, Al-Andalus was under the authority of the Almohad Caliphate. By this time, the Reconquista in Spain saw the takeover of several Muslim cities and territories, a development which further strained relations between Muslims and their non-Muslim counterparts, including the Jews. Breaking with the precedent of tolerance set by previous Muslim rulers, the Almohads imposed restrictions on the freedoms of non-Muslims and actively sought to convert them.

With such tolerance in Spain gradually fading for the Jews, Musa moved to Cairo, where he was introduced to Salahuddin. As a trained doctor, educated in perhaps the best centers of knowledge in the world, Musa's skills were taken with appreciation by the sultan, who hired him as his personal physician in the palace. Salahuddin also appointed Musa as the Nagid, a position for the chief Jewish community leaders, representing the Jews before a Muslim leader. He was now the acting representative of the Jewish people, within Salahuddin's administration.

In leading his synagogue in Cairo, Musa Ibn Maymun wrote extensive books and other works on philosophy. Within his writings, Musa was known to express a number of different philosophical perspectives alongside Jewish ethics, borrowing from Aristotle, Plato, and even Islam, in his takes on issues such as property, marriage, and other areas of secular life. His career, in theological and ethical matters, saw him become one of the first systematizers of Jewish law. In his Mishneh Torah, Musa compiled several important Jewish texts into one book, for the convenience of his followers, making him both a controversial and beloved figure in the Jewish tradition.

Despite the internal struggles and conflicts within the Muslim world, Jews contributed to the economic, cultural, scientific, and political development of various Muslim polities, from Cordoba in the West to Cairo in the East. Jews, alongside their Christian counterparts, played an integral component of this period of prosperity. Occupying various professions, in science, language, medicine, economics, and at times even in politics, the Jews, like the Christians, were just as responsible for the development of the Muslim world, as Muslims were themselves.

And when Salahuddin hired the services of men like Musa Ibn Maymun, he did so not only knowing that they had the minds to advance the development of his state, but that in giving them the opportunity, freedom, and respect that they deserved, he was following the precedent set by the Prophet Muhammad ﷺ and the first caliphs of Islam, such as Omar Ibn Khattab (رضي الله عنه). Thus, Salahuddin was modeling himself after those early Muslim statesmen, so that he, like them, would also prevail and be successful in governing a country.

Chapter 9
Two Sultans

Zengid Dirham from Sinjar (1210 - 1211)

"And if two groups of believers fight each other, then make peace between them. But if one of them transgresses against the other, then fight against the transgressing group until they are willing to submit to the rule of Allah. If they do so, then make peace between both in all fairness and act justly. Surely Allah loves those who uphold justice."

وَإِن طَآئِفَتَانِ مِنَ ٱلْمُؤْمِنِينَ ٱقْتَتَلُوا۟ فَأَصْلِحُوا۟ بَيْنَهُمَا ۖ فَإِنۢ بَغَتْ إِحْدَىٰهُمَا عَلَى ٱلْأُخْرَىٰ فَقَـٰتِلُوا۟ ٱلَّتِى تَبْغِى حَتَّىٰ تَفِىٓءَ إِلَىٰٓ أَمْرِ ٱللَّهِ ۚ فَإِن فَآءَتْ فَأَصْلِحُوا۟ بَيْنَهُمَا بِٱلْعَدْلِ وَأَقْسِطُوٓا۟ ۖ إِنَّ ٱللَّهَ يُحِبُّ ٱلْمُقْسِطِينَ

- Surah Al-Hujurat of the Quran (49:9)

From the beginning of Islamic history, when the Arabs expanded the borders of the caliphate across the known world, civil war and infighting have always paralyzed their efforts, leaving them susceptible to outside intervention. In 656, when the last of the first Islamic caliphs, Ali (رضي الله عنه) met in open battle with Muawiya Ibn Abi Sufyan, the governor of Syria, it sparked a civil war that weakened the integrity of the caliphate. In Constantinople, the Romans watched with excitement and sensed opportunity. Emperor Constans II wrote to Muawiya a letter, allegedly containing the following message:

"We know what occurred between you and Ali Ibn Abi Talib, and we see that you are more worthy of the caliphate. If you order me, I will send you an army that will bring you the head of Ali."

Muawiya's letter, based off of some Muslim sources, was reported to have detailed the following response to the Caesar of the Romans:

"Two brothers dispute, and what is it to you to enter between them? If you are not silent, I will send *you* an army that starts with you and ends with me, that will bring me *your head* so I can gift it to Ali."

After the assassination of Ali (رضي الله عنه) by Kharijite rebels, Muawiya would become caliph, the first of the Umayyads, and it would be he, who would be the first Muslim ruler to send an army to besiege Constantinople, Europe's largest city and the capital of the Romans. During the time of Salahuddin, a similar development, of tension between two Muslim leaders, was brewing. But it was not between the Sultan of Egypt and some rival Muslim ruler, who challenged him for his seat of authority. It was his old mentor, Sultan Nureddin Zengi, in Damascus.

In 1173, in the high mountains of Lebanon, Zengid troops marched through the land on a dark early morning, but as a defeated army. In that year, both sultans had committed themselves to war against the Crusaders, attacking them on both fronts, Syria in the north and Egypt in the south. Nureddin would advance on Tripoli and Salahuddin would attack the Kingdom of Jerusalem before the Zengids too would join him in liberating the holy city.

But of course, that did not actually happen. While Nureddin initiated his campaign against the Crusaders in the north, Salahuddin withdrew from participating in the campaign. In writing his excuse to the Zengid sultan, he explained that there was a rebellion in Cairo, redirecting his attention back to Egypt's domestic security concerns.

By this time, the young, ambitious Sultan of Egypt was 35 years old and had rebuilt his new country at an unprecedented pace, within only four years in office. And as a result of the numerous campaigns he launched into North Africa, Sudan, Hejaz, and Yemen, Egypt emerged from the ashes of the Fatimid Caliphate as the most powerful of the Islamic states with an economy and military that seemed to grow without end. As he rode his stallion through the streets of Cairo, the common people flocked to catch a glimpse of him, showering him with praise and admiration.

The rebellion, a seemingly minor threat, which called him back to Cairo, was all but deterred. It is unknown just how serious of a matter it was or if Salahuddin had calculated to not join the Zengid offensive, out of some broader strategy he put together, perhaps in an effort to bolster his own power against that of his former mentor.

The effects, however, would be immensely damaging to his relationship with the Zengid sultan. Nureddin had suspected that Salahuddin was plotting against him. Losing trust in his once loyal vassal, Nureddin assembled an army with the ultimate goal of launching a fourth Zengid expedition into Egypt, this time to dethrone Salahuddin.

Such a war would have been disastrous for both sides, as Nureddin's army would certainly have confronted significant challenges in defeating Salahuddin's Egyptian military. Both sides possessed enough manpower and resources to deplete each other in a long, drawn out war. It would have also given the Crusaders a chance to recover their forces and take advantage of the infighting.

Such a war, however, did not come to pass. On May 15th 1174, Sultan Nureddin Zengi died. Long after he was buried at his madrasa, in Damascus, Salahuddin received the news of his passing. Aside from the devastating personal loss for himself, as a close student and follower of the late sultan, Salahuddin was also troubled by another detail within the letter. The governor of Aleppo, Gumustekin Bey, had immediately taken advantage of the sultan's death, seizing his 11-year-old heir, As-Saleh Ismail, and enacting a plot to eliminate all the other rival emirs.

In Cairo, Salahuddin contemplated the disaster that had erupted in Damascus. His mind must have dwelled for hours on end. One would imagine how he remembered Nureddin and how glorious the days of his reign were. He remembered when he was six years old, how the then prince and his father rode together into the streets of Damascus after they had conquered Edessa for the Muslims. Nureddin was Salahuddin's hero, his teacher, his leader, and now he had left the world for the next one.

Chapter 10
Tremors in the Land

Citadel of Damascus, Syria

As Salahuddin watched from his capital in Egypt, he understood clearly that Nureddin had no true successor. The evidence of that was the disorder that unfolded after his passing. The governors of Syria's cities, acting out of their own interests, were tarnishing the legacy that Nureddin had left for the country to inherit. They threatened everything that the Muslim revival had built. And it was this chaos that Salahuddin knew obstructed the path to Al-Aqsa. Salahuddin very likely believed that only he could restore order to Damascus and rule Syria. The very heart of the Muslim world deserved to be headed by serious leadership, for only then could Greater Syria assume its place as the unifying force in the Ummah, redirecting it, its armies, its resources, its populations, its efforts back to the mission of revival and of ultimately reconquering Jerusalem.

The sultan was even recorded to have said, "When God gave me the country of Egypt, I was sure that He meant Palestine for me as well."

But instead of embarking immediately upon a swift and bloody campaign into Syria, Salahuddin waited. In this time, relations between Zengid Syria and Ayyubid Egypt began to suffer from the unruly emirs in Aleppo and Mosul. Governors like Gumustekin Bey began adopting harsher language when dealing with the sultan. Seeing him as the unruly defector, they slandered him as disloyal. He had only ascended to a position of authority in Egypt because of them. In their eyes, he, a Kurd, was obligated to remain subservient to his Turkic overlords.

Despite the apparent contempt for him by the ruling elite in Syria, Salahuddin remained in touch with his political values, seeing it as immoral to act with such open aggression against other Muslims. He needed a proper justification to march on Syria. For the time being, Salahuddin gave his support to the son of Nureddin, As-Saleh Ismail, promising the young boy that he would come to his aid if the need arose.

However, any plan of his to conquer Damascus, would be delayed by the emergence of a new threat against him. In the summer of 1174, Egypt was struck with a new Crusader attack. A naval fleet of Sicilian and Crusader vessels had laid siege to Alexandria. The second largest city in Egypt,

Alexandria, stood at the shores of the Mediterranean Sea to face the arrival of the naval invasion. Hoping to seize a beachhead that would serve in the conquest of the rest of the country, the Crusaders eyed it from their ships. Within their fleet were galleys, transport ships, and other vessels. The formidable force that the Crusaders assembled with their Sicilian allies formed a blockade, and they moved in slowly to disembark for the assault. This was not the first attack that they had launched upon Ayyubid Egypt.

In the past, Damietta was attacked by the Byzantine-Crusader coalition of 1169 and suffered heavy damage. But on this occasion, the sultan had prepared well for their arrival. Soldiers and supplies were quickly sent to Alexandria to reinforce the defenders. At first, the Ayyubids suffered heavy losses at the sea walls and many of the commercial and naval vessels of the Egyptians were sunk by the invaders. But Salahuddin's reinforcements quickly turned back the intruders, fighting them off the defenses of the city and launching barrages of arrows upon the approaching ships as well as bombarding them with siege weapons.

On that day, as more of the sultan's reinforcements arrived in the city, the morale of the defenders was greatly boosted. On the second day of the battle, when the Crusaders made their last stand with one final assault on the city's sea walls with their siege towers, the Ayyubid defenders met them on the defenses and fought them back, until the wind of the afternoon blew over the city when the battle ceased to go on any longer.

The corpses of the Crusaders were abandoned at Alexandria, while those who survived fled across the sea aboard what was left of their fleet. The Muslims burned down the siege towers they built, collected the weapons of the dead or captured knights, and succeeded in securing the city from the attackers. And it all took place in just three days. With the Crusader threat all but eliminated and no other obstacles standing in the gap before him, Salahuddin then turned to reorganize his army and prepare for his long-awaited invasion of Syria.

Chapter 11
Uniting the Realm

Sword of the Prophet Muhammad ﷺ, Topkapi Palace, Istanbul, Turkey

In January of 630, just 8 years after their migration to Medina, the Muslims, led by their Prophet ﷺ, returned to the holy city of Mecca, not as refugees, such as they once were, but as conquerors. In that year, in the middle of the month of Ramadan, the Prophet ﷺ led them back to the city they were once forced out of, where they were boycotted, marginalized, persecuted, harassed, bullied, and robbed for their belief in one God and their demands for a fairer society, based on the ideals of justice.

Many of the returning Muslims came from the lowest classes of Mecca, and they had experienced the worst of that society. The fear among the people of Mecca, the people of Quraysh, was that when the Muslims returned, they would act as all conquerors act, enacting revenge upon them. But they did not come with the desire of revenge. According to two hadith sources, the Prophet ﷺ told the people:

"Oh Quraysh, what do you think I will do to you?"

They replied, "You are a noble brother, son of a noble brother."

The Prophet ﷺ then said: "I say to you as Yusuf (Joseph) said to his brothers: 'No blame will there be upon you today. May Allah forgive you. He is the Most Merciful of the merciful.'"

"Go, for you are free."

- Prophet Muhammad ﷺ [Ibn Kathir, *Al-Bidaya wa'l-Nihaya*, Vol. 4]

It was this quality of the Sunnah that cemented the presence of the Muslims everywhere they went, from Mecca, to Jerusalem, and beyond. Forgiveness and mercy were prime characteristics of the Prophet ﷺ, and, every time the

Muslims, in times of war and peace, followed them properly, historically, their endeavours have ended in success.

In 1174, when Syria was embroiled within its own crisis, Salahuddin looked on with intentions to fulfill his conquest of that country. And, through his dedication to following the Sunnah, he understood that mercy and benevolence would earn him the hearts of the Syrian people. Great leaders do not conquer lands; they conquer hearts.

In July of 1174, with the sun shining overhead in the late afternoon, Salahuddin quickly mustered together 700 men for the long journey to Damascus. These 700 were the Mamluks, the sultan's elite soldiers. Taken from Turkic tribes from the Caucasus, the Steppe, and even some from Ukraine, they were brought to Egypt, raised as Muslims, and trained in the profession of combat and warfare. They were among the deadliest cavalry of their age, and Salahuddin would rely on them on this endeavor, as they would take him through foreign, unfriendly lands on the road to Damascus. The sultan rode his horse past the lines of his men, addressing them with an invigorating speech before they began the march. Answering the call of their leader, the Mamluks chanted with him, accelerating their steeds and taking off with their sultan.

Across the vast desert, Salahuddin and his Mamluk horsemen rode for Damascus. He and his companions had faced many traitors in the past. Salahuddin sought to make Gumustekin and the rest of his collaborators the last of them.

After racing through the Sinai desert, one obstacle remained in their way, the Crusaders. Upon entering the mountainous region east of the Jordan River, the Crusaders were already there, waiting for them, watching from afar. Salahuddin, seeking a faster route to reach Damascus, elected to pass through the Kingdom of Jerusalem. There were concerns, however, both among the Crusaders and among his own men over the safety of such a road, which was why the sultan requested to reach an agreement with the new king. Amalric I, who launched the Crusader invasions of Egypt in the 1160s had died. His son, Baldwin IV, a boy afflicted with leprosy, was now king.

After both leaders, Salahuddin and Baldwin, communicated through a dialogue of letters and messages, the Crusaders agreed to allow the sultan passage to Damascus. Salahuddin and his men thus traversed through Crusader territory, passing the cities of Kerak and Shobak, across Jordan's rough, hilly terrain, until both the Dead Sea and the Sea of Galilee were behind them. That was when they entered the borders of the Zengids. And soon, their horses would touch the soil of the mountain valley that Damascus lay in. In the fall of 1174, the sultan had reached Damascus, looking onward to the Syrian capital.

The walls of that city, which they gazed out towards, were lined with guards. The Zengid soldiers saw the eagle flags of the Ayyubids, hoisted proudly by the elite Mamluks in the plain to the south. Standing guard on the walls with his men was Farrukh Shah, the Governor of Baalbek and the nephew of Salahuddin through the sultan's brother, Nureddin Shahanshah. Farrukh Shah also brought his younger brother with him, Taqieddin Umar, a young man of a strong build, who accompanied his brother on the journey.

With the support of his nephews and multiple other Zengid officials, Salahuddin was granted entry. Seeing the gates unlocked for him, Salahuddin was relieved, as he would no longer need to take Damascus through any conflict, and the city was spared from bloodshed. He then led his men into the city.

Upon passing through the arched gateway, the people celebrated his arrival. The citizens in the streets cheered for him, welcoming the return of the great Muslim leader, who had grown in popularity in the hearts and minds of the Ummah. And as an example of his generosity, he had large sums of money distributed to the masses in an act of charity and of showing the people that he was grateful to see them. No resistance greeted the sultan on that day. Damascus was effectively delivered to him. Salahuddin also took possession of the citadel. The political turmoil, which had sent shockwaves through Syrian society, was now about to be addressed by this new sultan.

Just as the sultan's entrance won him legitimacy from the people of Damascus, through his evident exemplification of the same virtues of mercy and benevolence as those found in the Sunnah of the Prophet Muhammad ﷺ, one can only visualize the parallels between this 12th-century liberation of Damascus and the liberation of December 8th, 2024. On that day, the forces of the opposition, upon securing the capital of the nation, proclaimed that all citizens, regardless of their ethnic or religious backgrounds, were to be protected under the new order.

Many of these Syrian fighters, who freed Damascus on December 8th, once had homes in Midan, Darayya, and Ghouta. They, like the Sahaba that returned to Mecca, were forcibly displaced and were separated from their families, their property, and their entire livelihoods. And so when they returned in triumph, they assured the people that no harm would come to them. Among the people of Syria, the Sunnis, Shias, Alawites, Christians, Kurds, Turks, and Druze, all of them would be granted the promise of amnesty and protection by the opposition forces. They would not act with the same barbarity that the old regime had shown to them. It would be a day of mercy, of forgiveness, of peace.

And so, as Salahuddin concentrated his forces in Damascus and worked to gain control of all the various institutions of the old administration, he moved to make Damascus the capital of his state. His sultanate, which had possessed Egypt, Yemen, Mecca, Medina, and now Syria, would anchor its center of power in Damascus. From Syria, the sultan would govern his state, placing it at the center of the Muslim world. In organizing his circle of ministers and governors, the sultan had made his brother, Turanshah, governor of Damascus. After leaving Cairo and spending significant time in Yemen, Turanshah asked to be reassigned to the heart of the empire, rather than a distant province like Yemen. Thus, when Damascus was taken, Turanshah was given the responsibility of governing the capital of the state.

However, he also made another appointment. Imadeddin Al-Isfahani was a scribe and administrator, originally from Isfahan, Iran, who had been educated in the Nizamiyya Madrasa of Baghdad. He had served as vizier to Nureddin Zengi and had been reappointed to the same office by Salahuddin, effectively making him the prime minister of the state.

And to further bolster his legitimacy and forge robust ties with the rest of the old aristocracy of Damascus, the sultan married Ismatadin Khatun. From a noble family, she was the widow to the late Sultan Nureddin Zengi. And while she was 10 years older than Salahuddin, the sultan still married her, knowing that it would serve in the best interests of restoring stability to his rule over Syria. In many ways, she was the key to the success of his reign.

With his additional forces having reached the city from Egypt, the sultan shortly set out with them from Damascus to march north for the rest of his campaign, aiming to gain control of the rest of Syria, primarily its second largest city, Aleppo. His soldiers swept through the countryside, capturing town after town and advanced closer and closer to Aleppo. In the early spring of 1175, Salahuddin and his army were on the road to reach the city. And it was only a matter of time before all of Syria was his. From the day he arrived in Damascus, Baalbek, Homs, and Hama all surrendered to him. Aleppo would be next to submit.

But the Zengid remnants would not surrender their domains without resistance. To the east, the army from Mosul trekked across the terrain to confront the sultan and stop his advance. Commanding the right wing of the army was Muzafferidin Gökbörü. Gökbörü was the son of Emir Zainuddin Ali Kutçek, the former Zengid governor of Erbil. He was a young commander, but determined as ever to crush the perceived enemy. He saw Salahuddin's conquest for power as a betrayal, aimed at the ailing Zengid state. At the head of this coalition of Zengid cities was the brother of Sayfaddin Ghazi Ibn Mawdud, Izzaddin Mas'ud.

Gökbörü commanded a contingent of Turkoman cavalry, among which he was considered as one of the fiercest. This contingent, which made up a third of Sayfaddin Ghazi's coalition, together with the rest of the army commanded by the Emir of Mosul, continued its march towards Hama. And soon enough, they entered a field, elevated in the hilly terrain, several miles outside the city of Hama, known as the Horns of Hama.

On the opposite side of the plain, the sultan and his army stood waiting for them in their battle formation. The 10,000 strong coalition, assembled at the behest of Mosul, was more than a match for the Ayyubid army that had come from Damascus. Salahuddin, however, was prepared. On his left flank, he gave command to his nephew, Taqieddin Umar, and on his right, he gave authority of those troops to Farrukh Shah. He would lead the first contingent himself. The sultan, with his brother, Turanshah, by his side, commanding from the center, dispatched a message to the Zengid army, offering them a chance to surrender and avoid the toll that battle takes. When this was rejected, he ordered the attack. All at once, the army charged across the plain to meet their Zengid opponents in the field. The two armies clashed. Both sides fought fiercely with their leaders joining them in battle. But soon enough, the engagement had turned into a standstill. Seeing this, Gökbörü seized the initiative and led his troops on the right flank of his army to attack the Ayyubid left wing, which he perceived to be the most vulnerable. He entered battle with his Turkoman riders and engaged their opponents. The Ayyubid cavalry attempted to repel this charge, but the wave that Gökbörü unleashed broke the defense of that section.

    Near to where this attack had taken place, the sultan saw how his nephew lost control of his left flank, and so he raced towards that section with a number of Mamluk cavalrymen. As Gökbörü planned to finish his defeated opponent, he witnessed the sultan himself and several heavily armed Ayyubid riders descend down upon him like a tidal wave. It was futile. They had trapped and surrounded him. Gökbörü surrendered.

The psychological shock from the arrival of the Mamluks routed the rest of his men. They were chased down by the Ayyubid cavalry and were either captured or slain in the field. As for the rest of the Zengid army, some were taken prisoners, while others deserted into the wilderness. Izzaddin Mas'ud and Gökbörü were both arrested by the sultan and were brought to him, as he sat on his horse and overlooked the field that was the Horns of Hama.

In Aleppo, Gumustekin received the cold news of the defeat of Mosul's army. Sayfaddin's brother as well as Gökbörü were both taken prisoner. It was now certain that Aleppo would be tested with a siege. What made the daunting task of defending Aleppo far more challenging for the Zengid emir and the few allies with him was the assembly of siege weapons by the Ayyubids. When the sun finally set on Aleppo and its surroundings descended into darkness, the siege began. Hundreds of engineers and laborers prepared the sultan's siege engines to fire. Then suddenly, flaming projectiles of rock, tar, and fire were launched at the city by Salahuddin's newly acquired siege weapon, the trebuchet, a tall and massive machine, capable of sending cannonades high into the sky before crashing down upon the enemy beneath. Aleppo's defenses were bombarded by these weapons, and the battle would see the Zengid guardians of the city try to survive the constant fire by their Ayyubid besiegers.

However, Gunustekin would attempt a maneuver to save him and his city from being conquered by Salahuddin's army. One night, as the sultan's forces continued to besiege the city, a man had found him in his tent. This lone figure rushed inside with a dagger in his hand and attempted to kill the sultan. Very nearly did that dagger sink itself into Salahuddin's chest, but his Mamluks, immediately upon being alarmed by the commotion, moved to save their leader. The assailant was slain, and the assassination was thwarted. Such a breach in his army's security became deeply disturbing to the sultan and his commanders. Measures were taken to tighten movements within the camp, and an investigation was conducted into the identity of the attacker. They had soon discovered that he was sent by the Order of Assassins, a sect of killers, and their leader, Rashidadin Sinan.

This Sinan, the *old man of the mountain* as he was called, ruled from Masyaf Castle. According to legend, the order's men were once boys, who were taken from their villages, drugged, purged of any weakness, and trained to serve and kill for their brotherhood. While their castles ruled the high, cold cliffs of the north, the assassins did not belong to the land. A century earlier, they were banished from Egypt. Their leader, Imam Al-Nizar, was murdered by rival heirs of the Fatimid Caliphate. And so his followers left and set out to plant their creed in the north, thus they migrated to Syria and built their castles.

The Sunni states of the region interpreted their presence to be an Ismaili conspiracy, a network plotting to undermine their rule. Many would challenge the Nizari-Ismailis. The Abbasid caliph in Baghdad waged war against them, only for him and his sons to be assassinated in cold blood. The Seljuk Sultan of Rûm also confronted the Assassins but was forced to abandon the campaign when the assassins snuck into the tent of his war camp and left a dagger on his bed, threatening him with the very real possibility of returning and planting another dagger into his chest. The Assassins had killed princes and kings, severed the heads of dynasties, and now their plots were aimed at Salahuddin, allegedly now in collaboration with Gumustekin Bey.

After the assassination attempt in the sultan's camp, Salahuddin ordered his army to besiege Masyaf Castle. During the stalemate, the sultan hosted in his tent a messenger from the castle to discuss terms for its surrender. It was there that it was revealed that two of Salahuddin's bodyguards had been assassins of the order and had been embedded as sleeper cells in his army. A dagger, laced with poison, was also found in the sultan's sleeping quarters. This shock led the sultan to make terms with Sinan, leading to the end of the siege and the withdrawal of his army from Masyaf Castle.

Turning his attention back on Aleppo, the sultan would move to diplomatically gain at least influence over the city, instead of completely laying siege and leaving it in ruins.

In a correspondence with As-Saleh Ismail, Nureddin's heir, whom Gumustekin had held custody over since 1174, the sultan attempted to persuade him to dispose of Gumustekin. Finally with the support of Salahuddin and some Zengid officials against Gumustekin, As-Saleh Ismail would demand that the emir cede territory back to him and resign from his position. When this offer was refused, Gumustekin was arrested and executed outside the walls of Aleppo.

With Gumustekin dead and As-Saleh Ismail left to govern with a degree of autonomy, Aleppo would slowly become part of Salahuddin's expanding state. This lasted until 1183, when Salahuddin gained control of the city through diplomatic measures, effectively securing northern Syria without ever needing to conquer the city itself. However, Gumustekin's reign of instability did not come to an end without making one final attempt against Salahuddin. In 1176, he agreed to a prisoner ransom with the Crusaders of Antioch, releasing one Reynald de Châtillon, who had been imprisoned in Aleppo's citadel by Nureddin Zengi for over 15 years. Despite Mosul, cities of the Jazira region, and Iraq yet to submit, the sultan had succeeded in his project of bringing Egypt, Arabia, and Syria under the rule of his state. His borders encompassed vast stretches of the Middle East, and his state was easily the most powerful and feared entity in the region since the days of the old Abbasid Caliphate. The sultan's gaze of conquest had now turned westward, upon the Crusader states and Jerusalem itself.

Part III
Liberation
(1177 - 1187)

16th-century Turkish Cavalry Armor
Museum of Islamic Art in Doha, Qatar

Murad 104

Chapter 12
Shattered

Coin of Baldwin IV (1173 - 1185)

Across the Red Sea, the heartland of Salahuddin's dominion awaited his return from Syria. That year in 1177, he had completed his campaign in the Levant to secure Damascus, Baalbek, Homs, and Hama as well as setting the stage to make a vassal out of Aleppo. He had spared the Zengids in the north and turned his eyes towards the Crusader kingdoms and Jerusalem itself.

But in 1177, the uncle of the 16-year-old King Baldwin IV, Philip of Flanders, arrived in the Holy Land with ambitions of his own. Taking most of the boy king's army with him, he departed Jerusalem to besiege Hama. However, instead of reacting with haste to defend this city of his in Syria, the sultan saw an opportunity in the vulnerable kingdom. The sultan had long made it his mission to liberate Jerusalem, which had been lost for nearly eight decades. He also weighed the security risk that came as the result of the prisoner ransom in Aleppo, which had led to the release of many dangerous Crusaders back to their lands, among them was Reynald de Châtillon. Driven by the perceived opportunity and strengthened geographically with the addition of Syria to his state, Salahuddin returned to Cairo to raise another army to strike the Crusaders.

In the citadels, fortresses, and castles that guarded Cairo, troops were being assembled and stockpiles of armor, weapons, and equipment were gathered. But such a movement of weapons at this scale could not go unnoticed. Eyes were watching. And word traveled fast. News had reached the king's ears in Jerusalem. Baldwin had summoned his advisers and commanders. Count Raymond III of Tripoli, Reynald de Châtillon, and a crowd of knights had come to his court to discuss the news of the sultan's impending attack on the kingdom.

In Egypt, the sultan's army was complete. And it was one of the largest armies he had ever assembled for a campaign, a total of 26,000 men, 8,000 of them being the elite Mamluks. Al-Adil remained and would not accompany his brother to war, as he would stay to govern the capital. Salahuddin, Taqieddin, and his other commanders climbed their horses and left. The sultan took command of his 26,000 strong army, and together they all raced across the land, crossing into the Sinai Peninsula, and traveling north to the Kingdom of Jerusalem.

Out of the desert, they emerged onto a plain that spanned from Gaza to Bir As-Saba'. At this time, the Crusader army of King Baldwin IV had entered the region of southern Palestine to meet the sultan's arrival. Riding behind the king was Reynald de Châtillon. He and the Templars had arrived with their knights and found Salahuddin's army marching north into their domain. The Crusaders only brought with them 3,000 infantrymen and 500 knights, vastly outnumbered by the Ayyubids. Salahuddin ignored their supposedly meager presence and urged his commanders to press the advance. They would take the towns of Darum and Gaza, before aiming for Askalan.

Taqieddin, the sultan's nephew and most senior commander, followed the instructions of his uncle. He took several thousand riders with him and rode north to these cities scattered along the coast. They spread out across the countryside and raided the farmlands to stir panic amongst the people of the land. The sultan's men attacked Crusader defenses and severed their supply lines. Their raids left behind scores of victims, burned settlements, and demolished fortifications. And when they reached Darum and Gaza, Taqieddin had his men occupy the castles of those cities and raise their flags, securing them for the Ayyubids.

Even a small division of the army had reached as far as

Ramallah, only a few miles from Jerusalem. The sultan's hands had reached deep into the Crusader kingdom, and it seemed for a moment that Al-Aqsa would be theirs. However, their spree would not go without facing its consequences. Askalan withstood the Ayyubid onslaught, for the Muslims were unable to advance into the fortified city. And coming from the north, an ever growing Crusader presence was gathering in the region, answering the call of King Baldwin IV. Salahuddin, who had his army camped outside the village of Ramla, was left without a great portion of his army. He had spread his forces dangerously thin, and it was a mistake. The wind was beginning to blow against him.

Then on one afternoon, on November 25th, 1177, his men came under fire from a barrage of arrows. The clouded sky rained volleys upon them, inflicting great damage and igniting fear within the sultan's army. Salahuddin, who had been planning his advance on Jerusalem from the towns his army captured, emerged from his tent to find himself in the midst of chaos and violence. The army of Jerusalem had attacked, and his men were most unprepared. With his armor on his body and his sword unsheathed from its scabbard, the sultan raced out into the field with his Mamluks.

Charging towards him were several waves of knights, who, protected under heavy armor and charging with strong horses, smashed the Ayyubid frontline. Riding down the hill, the teenage King Baldwin IV charged furiously on his horse, mustering great strength and bravery, as he attacked and fought off numerous Muslim fighters. Placing a great deal of trust in their young king, the knights followed his charge across the plain that became the graveyard of thousands of Salahuddin's soldiers.

The sultan understood that the terrain was unsuitable and so he instructed his men to regroup at the hill of Ramla, a site known to the Crusaders as *Montgisard*. Salahuddin, protected by his Mamluks, gathered a great number of troops and retreated to the safety of Montgisard. The Crusaders followed them there. It was futile. The hill's highground would not save him. Upon facing the arrival of the Crusaders, the sultan's lines broke. His soldiers began to flee. However, he would stand firm with his Mamluks in the face of the Crusader onslaught. In the midst of the chaotic fighting, after the sultan himself had slain one of the knights, another danger came for him.

One bold Templar, who charged on his horse towards the sultan, leaped from his mount and launched himself through the air with his sword aiming for the sultan. Salahuddin looked up to see the very tip of the blade within mere striking distance of his face. But then one of his most loyal Mamluks had rushed to his aid, stopping the sword of that Templar with his shield. He had thwarted this attempt on his leader's life and fought him off, until he broke the knight's defense and cut him down.

Seeing the danger that had flooded through the cracks of the sultan's security, Salahuddin was advised by his

Mamluks to escape. He agreed, and with them, he fled from the battle. After retreating from Montgisard, they were chased for miles by the knights of the Baldwin IV, until they eventually gave up their pursuit and returned to their side of the border. Montgisard had been a disaster.

Chapter 13
Reversing the Wind

Krak des Chevaliers, Al-Husn, Syria

"And whoever puts their trust in Allah, then He alone will be enough for them. Certainly Allah achieves His Will. Allah has already set a destiny for everything."

وَمَن يَتَوَكَّلْ عَلَى ٱللَّهِ فَهُوَ حَسْبُهُۥ ۚ إِنَّ ٱللَّهَ بَٰلِغُ أَمْرِهِۦ ۚ قَدْ جَعَلَ ٱللَّهُ لِكُلِّ شَىْءٍ قَدْرًا

- Surah Al-Talaq of the Quran (65:3)

    With 2,000 Mamluks riding with him, Salahuddin witnessed the sun's light penetrate into the dark world, from which he had escaped. For days, the sultan and his men were lost in the Sinai desert, wandering through a barren terrain, from which they could find no way out of. They were trapped.

From Cairo, Qadi Al-Fadil learned of the sultan's precarious situation, and so he dispatched a group of Bedouin Arabs to rescue him. They traveled at full speed to locate their leader, and, through their expertise in navigating the desert wilderness, they succeeded in finding and guiding him back to Cairo.

The Battle of Montgisard was a humiliating catastrophe for the sultan and had shattered the expectations that Jerusalem would be liberated in the near future. He returned to Cairo with a meager tenth of his army, only 2,000 men. Over 20,000 others did not make it back to Cairo, suffering a far more grim fate at the field of Montgisard. The geopolitical consequences that would arise, out of Salahuddin's disastrous defeat at Montgisard, would far outweigh any of the sultan's emotional damage or personal humiliation.

At 16, Baldwin IV, a boy struggling with leprosy, had surmounted all expectations on his abilities to protect Jerusalem. At Montgisard, he proved to the world what kind of leader he would be, as he shattered and utterly crushed Salahuddin's massive army like the proper warrior king. Some chroniclers even drew parallels between him and David when he slew Goliath. As for the sultan, he was made dangerously vulnerable, his projection of power over the realms of the Muslims hung by a thread, and moreover any aspirations of conquering Jerusalem were entirely suspended for the foreseeable future.

Across the Sinai desert, the lords of the Kingdom of Jerusalem celebrated their triumph over the sultan. It was Christmas, and the Crusader kingdom was in celebration that it had been saved. Victory parades were held in streets, unveiling the spoils of battle. And at the royal court, Baldwin IV rested with pride on his throne, above the stone steps that overlooked the grand hall. In the early spring of 1178, Baldwin would give his permission to Reynald, the Knights Templar, and many other hawkish Crusader lords to unleash a new wave of raids against towns and villages in Syria. They attacked, plundered, and pillaged, meeting little opposition to their storm of violence.

In Egypt, news of these crimes reached Cairo, putting the sultan under intense pressure to return to Syria to force the raiding to end. In his war chambers, he consulted his generals and strategized a counterattack. With time and resources moving against him, the sultan was able to muster a few thousand soldiers and elite Mamluks to take him back to the Levant. They raced across the desert, just as the sultan had done before. In Damascus, Turanshah, Farrukh Shah, and Imadeddin Al-Isfahani welcomed him back to the Syrian capital. Upon descending from his horse, he immediately demanded an assessment of the security situation of the city.

Anticipating the Crusaders to make for Damascus and lay siege, the sultan appointed his nephew, Farrukh Shah, as the garrison commander. Turanshah would be reassigned to Baalbek, as its governor. As for the sultan himself, he planned to take on another mission. His spies reported to him of a castle that the Crusaders were building in the Golan Heights. Once completed, it would give the Crusaders a territorial advantage that would threaten the trade routes, connecting Damascus to the Hejaz provinces of the Red Sea, Jeddah, Mecca, Medina, Yemen, and out to the Indian Ocean. The sultan aimed to raise this stronghold to the ground.

However, yet more news had come to the ears of the sultan. A messenger reported to him that the Zengid emirs of Mosul and the Jazira region had once again taken to rebellion. Their treason, in the eyes of the sultan, had to be dealt with, but he could not be everywhere. The sultan had a vast array of commanders willing to secure the cities of the region for him and bring them fully under his authority. He would have to delegate certain missions to them to complete on their own, while he focused on the Crusader threat.

To the west, in the Golan Heights, the Crusaders were building their castle on a mountain peak known as *Jacob's Ford*. Despite most sections of the castle remaining under construction, it was already being used for military operations. From there, as Reynald and the Knights Templar both strategized their raids on the trade routes, the army of Jerusalem marched out towards Damascus for the siege on the city. The king, accompanied by his guardian, Count Raymond III of Tripoli, led the army before the city and expected little resistance.

In Hama, however, Salahuddin's forces under Taqieddin crushed the Crusader incursion upon the city. The skirmishes, which broke out to the north of Damascus, were quelled with the sultan's response, aided with the efforts of Farrukh Shah in Baalbek. And finally, when Baldwin's army arrived outside Damascus, the Ayyubid army led by Salahuddin met them in battle. They fought intensely in the fields south of the city, and ultimately they defeated Franks and sent them into retreat.

Salahuddin had turned the tide of the war and regained his authority over the region. Montgisard had now become a distant memory. With the Crusaders expelled from Syria and their raids kept at bay, morale across the sultan's state was high. And to solidify his authority even further, the reinforcements from Egypt had finally come. And in 1179, he would then set his sights on seizing the Golan. After offering Baldwin 100,000 dinars for the castle at Jacob's Ford, the sultan's offer was soundly rejected.

And thus, under the cover of night, in the mountains of the Golan Heights, Salahuddin and his army arrived outside the castle of Jacob's Ford. The night was deep. Not a single fire had been lit in the sultan's army, which surrounded the castle. After assessing the situation, the sultan gave the order. The defenders of Jacob's Ford witnessed the sultan reveal himself and begin the siege on their fortifications.

His catapults and trebuchets pounded the walls and battered the ramparts throughout the entire night. The defenders struggled to survive under the bombardment, which continued for almost a week. And by the time the morning of the sixth day had nearly come, the second stage of the sultan's plan was progressing towards completion. Beneath the ground, his miners were digging a tunnel from their camp all the way to the walls of the castle. When it was finished, they loaded the end of the tunnel with hundreds of pounds of explosives. The tunnel was emptied and on the sultan's orders, the bomb was detonated.

That morning, when the Frankish defenders woke to the sixth day of the siege, the ground rumbled beneath them, until the entire eastern side of the wall suddenly collapsed at the explosion that erupted from beneath the ground. And when the dust had settled, an opening in the castle's defenses was revealed, a gap. With the sun rising to signal their attack, the Muslims charged for the breakthrough. Their thunderous screams echoed across the land, until they finally crashed upon the castle and battled their way inside. Several miles away, Crusaders from Jerusalem were sent to bring reinforcements to the castle. But when they arrived, they witnessed the eagle flags of the Ayyubids flying over the towers of the castle. They had come too late. They had no choice, but to abandon their mission and return to their king.

The sultan entered the courtyard of the castle and was delivered the victory of his soldiers, who proudly raised his flag into the sky and saluted him as they received him on the grounds, which they had conquered from the enemy. And thus, the Levantine war, which lasted from Montgisard in 1177 to Jacob's Ford in 1179, ended with the sultan surmounting the high ground and reasserting his image of strength over the region.

And what Salahuddin so evidently proved to the Crusaders was the true nature of war with the Muslims. Unlike the Latins, who constantly needed reinforcements and support from Europe, the Muslims were fighting on their home terrain, where they could sustain loss after loss and still continue to persist, until they prevailed.

Chapter 14
The Raider

Kerak Castle, Jordan

"Even united, they would not dare fight you except from within fortified strongholds or from behind walls. Their malice for each other is intense: you think they are united, yet their hearts are divided. That is because they are a people of no sense."

لَا يُقَاتِلُونَكُمْ جَمِيعًا إِلَّا فِى قُرًى مُّحَصَّنَةٍ أَوْ مِن وَرَآءِ جُدُرٍۢ ۚ بَأْسُهُم بَيْنَهُمْ شَدِيدٌ ۚ تَحْسَبُهُمْ جَمِيعًا وَقُلُوبُهُمْ شَتَّىٰ ۚ ذَٰلِكَ بِأَنَّهُمْ قَوْمٌ لَّا يَعْقِلُونَ

- Surah Al-Hashr of the Quran (59:14)

The loss of Jacob's Ford shook the very sense of

security within the Kingdom of Jerusalem and the surrounding Latin states. That castle, which they had erected to be an arrow aimed at both Salahuddin's Greater Syria and the holy cities of Mecca and Medina, was taken in just six days in 1179. At the royal court of Baldwin IV, the king summoned his advisers to demand an explanation for what had occurred and a solution to what was yet to come. Reynald de Châtillon, who, along with the Templars, had been a strong advocate for further conflict with the sultan, had his proposition for war refused.

Baldwin had elected to follow the advice of Count Raymond of Tripoli, who by now actedas the second most influential figure in the Kingdom of Jerusalem. Raymond could speak and write Arabic, thus making him central to Baldwin's diplomacy with Damascus. But like his rival, Raymond, Reynald had another ally in the kingdom, and it was perhaps, in some ways, a more powerful entity than the king himself.

The Knights Templar had operated in the Holy Land from the beginning of the founding of the Crusader states. Their order of knights functioned as both a military force and a financial organization. In Europe, a merchant could cash a check with the Knights Templar at one of their banks, travel to the Holy Land, and conclude his transaction in Jerusalem. This, together with their connections in Europe and the Holy Land, made the Templars perhaps the first international economic enterprise. They were the first true vehicle of a

European colonial endeavor, long before the Dutch or British East India Companies.

The reason why they took on the name, "the Knights Templar," was because their headquarters, along with much of the religious symbolism of their order, was located on the Temple Mount, *Templum Solomonis* as they called it, the compound of Masjid Al-Aqsa. In occupying the third holiest place of the Muslims, the grounds of Al-Aqsa, the Templars asserted themselves not just as the protectors of Christian pilgrims in the Holy Land, but as the triumphant bulwark of the Crusader enterprise against Islam.

While Reynald de Châtillon was not a knight, but a nobleman among the Franks in the Holy Land, he shared many of the same hawkish sentiments as the Templars. While there were some Crusaders like Raymond, who assumed that Salahuddin, like all other Muslim rulers, could be negotiated with, persuaded, even perhaps bribed, Reynald and the Templars adhered to a different analysis. They understood that this sultan would not stop, until Jerusalem was in his hands. For that reason, no diplomacy would suffice.

In 1183, Reynald along with his knights rode their horses deep into the rural lands of the Arabs. On the grounds of villages and date farms, they murdered and pillaged hundreds of residents. They ravaged farms, carelessly slaughtered livestock, burned down homes, and attacked travelers and merchants passing by. The raids would only escalate, as Reynald continued to drive deeper into

Salahuddin's territory, attacking the Hajj pilgrim routes to Mecca and Medina. These attacks left scores dead and the image of the security of the state crippled.

While Salahuddin would respond with retaliatory measures in light of these raids, in the months prior, he had long enjoyed months of peace, since he concluded his last military engagement with the Crusaders in the Golan. The people of Syria enjoyed the economic benefits of commerce returning from Egypt, and the image of their sultan was respected. In 1180, Salahuddin was presented with a letter. The news was of the passing of his older brother, Turanshah, in Alexandria. He had sent him there after the war ended to assume charge over the city, as its governor. For the sultan, the loss of his brother was a difficult affliction. Turanshah's body would be transferred to Damascus, where Salahuddin's sister, Fatima Sitt Al-Sham, buried him at her madrasa, Al-Shamiyah Al-Kubra. For the sultan, family and those he could trust were central to his life and his administration. His nephew, Taqieddin, had been given the city of Hama. Farrukh Shah, as governor of Damascus, was also given Baalbek after Turanshah's passing. But with the loss of one brother, Salahuddin would gain another.

In 1182, one man, who had proven his mettle in battle, would offer his support to the sultan. Muzafferidin Gökbörü, the Turkoman commander that rebelled against the sultan with the other Zengid emirs at Hama, approached Salahuddin, volunteered to help his army cross the Euphrates

River, and offered to lead them to secure the Jazira region. Gökbörü himself was from Erbil, one of the major cities of the area, and naturally would be a capable commander in establishing the sultan's order there. Salahuddin agreed and charged Gökbörü with the campaign.

But in 1185, when Izzaddin Mas'ud, the Zengid ruler of Mosul, revolted and became a serious concern to the sultan, Salahuddin launched a campaign against him himself. That year Gökbörü had promised a large sum of money to partially fund Salahuddin's military logistics in the region. When he failed to deliver, the sultan, already suspecting collusion with his former allies, the Zengids, had Gökbörü arrested. But during the campaign, when the sultan fell ill, Gökbörü hosted him at his castle in Harran. After the sultan recovered with the help of the medical treatment provided to him by Gökbörü's servants, Salahuddin forgave him and his trust was regained.

When the campaign ended, Gökbörü's efforts succeeded in bringing Mosul, Erbil, and its surroundings under the rule of the sultanate, as vassal cities of the sultan. In rewarding him for his loyalty, Salahuddin would grant Gökbörü the cities of Samsat and Urfa, formerly Edessa, both in southern Anatolia, near Harran. But also, he would reward him with the hand of his sister, Rabia Khatun. And thus Gökbörü, Salahuddin's best commander, became his brother-in-law. But just a few years earlier, in 1183, the sultan faced much more challenging circumstances with his relationship with the Crusaders.

As he ruled his state from Damascus, Salahuddin, having benefited from his treaty of peace with the Crusaders, allowing him time to focus on uniting the region, had finally been put under pressure by renewed Latin incursions. As Reynald de Châtillon pillaged and looted in the lands of the Arabs, he allegedly boasted that he would sack Medina and steal the body of the Prophet Muhammad ﷺ. Such an egregious aim would never of course materialize. Reynald's raids on land never reached Medina. And the Crusader fleet, that he sent to plunder the Red Sea coast, were intercepted and sunk by Salahuddin's naval forces, under the direction of his Mamluk commander, Husameddin Lulu. Husameddin would go on to capture the city of Aila, the Crusader's port city to the Red Sea, and even chased one of Reynald's raiding parties so far that they became exhausted, disembarked, fled across the desert, and were still apprehended by Husameddin's men. Despite these victories at sea, Salahuddin was compelled by his sense of duty to retaliate on land.

In 1183, in light of the devastation caused by Reynald's raids, the sultan decided on his course of action. One morning, the darkness of the sky began to turn to a lighter blue, as the sunrise drew near. It was Fajr, and Salahuddin had finished his prayer. That morning, atop the high walls of the citadel, the sultan stood tall, awaiting his commanders to be summoned to his presence. He stared off into the distance, keeping a watchful eye on the mountains and the lands that lay behind them. That day, Salahuddin and his army embarked upon the road to Kerak. They marched across the desert and vowed to raise it to the ground.

In Jerusalem, panic swept through the streets, as unrest amongst the people swelled and soldiers were assembled to both quell the anger and prepare to defend the kingdom. At the castle, a meeting was organized by Count Raymond for the king. Guy de Lusignan, once a newly arrived Frankish noble, now lord of Askalan and Jaffa, attended, as well as a great number of Templars, Hospitallers, and other orders allied with the two lords. Before all of them, Baldwin, in light of the actions of Reynald de Châtillon, in flagrant violation of the treaty, was forced to rush to the side of his vassal at Kerak.

Outside the walls of Kerak, the first phase of the conflict was yet to begin. Reynald de Châtillon returned to the security of his castle, where he would man the defense. All across the countryside, Arab riders conducted reconnaissance missions for the approaching army, which soon revealed itself in the year 1183. Atop the distant hill, where the Ayyubid army waited, the sultan was briefed in his tent.

Moments later, in the shadows of the sand blowing across the desert, Salahuddin and his entire force embarked upon the path towards their enemy. The catapults and trebuchets were moved into position before the walls of Kerak, and the sultan initiated the beginning of the siege. His artillery fired and pounded the defenses of Kerak for days. They fired day and night. The sultan made attempts to breach the walls, but all were repelled decisively by Reynald's men. Within days, the army of Jerusalem arrived after crossing the Jordan River. Due to the logistical difficulties of continuing the siege, the arrival of Baldwin's army, and the setbacks of the siege on Kerak, Salahuddin withdrew. A peace treaty was formulated and agreed upon by both the king and the sultan. Baldwin would attempt to reprimand Reynald de Châtillon, but to little long-term effect. In truth, Baldwin was incapable of enforcing the law over his vassals. And while the sultan's brief siege of Kerak had, in effect, dissuaded the Crusaders from launching further raids into the Hejaz for the time being, it did not completely extinguish the threat that they constituted.

    For the sultan's army, Kerak had become yet another campaign into the Kingdom of Jerusalem, that ended without capturing the prize that was the holy city itself. Many of his commanders, like Taqieddin, believed that such exhaustive campaigns were unnecessary at this point. For them, the sultan's show of force against the Crusaders was enough. And geopolitically, there was already so much to be proud of. Salahuddin ruled Egypt, Syria, Yemen, northern Iraq, portions of North Africa, and the holy cities of Mecca and Medina. The region had not been led and unified by such a powerful state like this in centuries. But for Salahuddin, even this was not enough.

He often lamented at the state of the wider Muslim world. As his eyes wandered across the maps of his cartographers, he could only imagine how all of it, from the Atlantic shores of Spain to the frontiers of China, was Muslim land. The borders of Islam had encompassed virtually half of the known world, with most of the achievements of this expansion owing themselves to the Umayyad Caliphate, when Syria was the capital of Ummah. Having returned the center of leadership back to Syria, Salahuddin also had aspirations, like the caliphs before him, to spread Islam throughout the world. From the writings of his biographers, he thought a great deal about taking Islam deep into Europe. Constantinople and Rome certainly rested within the imagination of the Muslims at the time, as they did with their sultan, who often prayed especially for the conquest of Constantinople to come true.

But from the Atlantic to China, these Muslim polities were all disunited from one another. In the far west, the Almohad Caliphate ruled Spain and North Africa, often forced to contend with the Spanish kingdoms of Castile, Aragon, and Leon, at a time when the Reconquista was still very much alive. While Salahuddin bordered the Almohads in North Africa, there was little support they could lend him. To the north, the Seljuk Sultanate of Rûm ruled Anatolia. To the east, was the state of the Shirvanshahs in Azerbaijan, the

Abbasid Caliphate in Iraq, the Seljuk Empire in Iran, and the Khwarezmian Empire and Kara-Khoja Khanate in the Central Asian Steppe. In India, the lands around Delhi, along with parts of Afghanistan, Sindh, and Punjab, were ruled by the Ghurids.

All of these states and their rulers were completely absent from the war that Salahuddin was waging on their behalf. Some certainly had the means to support the sultan and were aware of his efforts in the Levant, but none of them came to aid him. Al-Aqsa's place was and still is central to Islamic heritage, for it is a site and a representation of a legacy that was honored upon the Muslims. At the sight of its loss to the Latins and simultaneously the disunity that crippled the Ummah from within, Salahuddin could only sit with frustration, knowing that he was the only Muslim ruler striving to liberate it for the Muslim world.

And so when his commanders voiced similar sentiments, that all his efforts had been enough, that he should rest, that he should instead suspend all immediate military action and focus on domestic affairs for the rest of his reign, the sultan would reply to them with an answer that completely illustrated his worldview, one which differed greatly from the rest of his contemporary Muslim leaders and even some of his exhausted commanders.

He would reply to them with, "How can I smile? How can food and drink taste good when Al-Aqsa is in the hands of the Crusaders

Chapter 15
A New King

Coin of Guy de Lusignan, Kingdom of Cyprus (1192 - 1194)

In Jerusalem, the sun had set over the holy city. King Baldwin's health, as a result of his leprosy, began to show serious signs of deterioration, forcing him to be confined to his bed and seek the care of his physicians. In Damascus, Salahuddin returned to his residence as well. His truce with the Franks had been reached, delaying the war that was still inevitable. But this false sense of peace would produce further consequences in the near future. As both sides returned to the domestic affairs of their respective countries, they soon bore the brunt of a wave of disease.

In 1185, plague had spread in Damascus. The city was terribly afflicted by infections amongst the various corners of its urban population. Entire neighborhoods and quarters of the city were deeply affected, leading to job vacancies and thus a period of decreased economic activity. But with the infrastructure and resources of Syria's capital, among them its hospitals, physicians, food supply, and administrative centers, Dasmscus emerged from the 1185 plague epidemic.

In Jerusalem, however, the king would not prevail in his battle with his own illness. Surrounded by his family and vassals, Baldwin IV, in the spring of 1185, died at the age of 24. His death marked the loss of one of the most powerful kings among the Crusaders, revered by the Chrsitians for his devoutness in his faith and his courage on the battlefield. After his death in 1185, the son of his sister, Baldwin V, would be enthroned as his successor. However, within a year, this boy too would succumb to the fate he inherited from his family line. Leprosy had killed him as well.

With the heirs of the throne of Jerusalem all dead, the path to rulership was now open to Guy de Lusignan, the lord of Askalan and Jaffa and husband to Princess Sibylla. In 1186, his coronation was held. Raymond, who himself tried to wrest the throne from Guy, was ultimately forced to submit before his new king. Reynald de Châtillon and the Templars were exonerated and were given high seats at the ceremony, smiling proudly at the sight of the crown being placed upon their ally's head. Guy had become king, and with his Templar allies standing loyally beside him, war lay only beyond the horizon. Those disillusioned with Guy's promises of holy war,

Raymond among them, watched in silence, unable to avert what was yet to befall them.

In his war camp, Salahuddin rested on his bed. While the sultan encamped with his army, the winter weather afflicted him with a cold, and he lay weak and exhausted inside his tent. One night, he received the news of Baldwin's death, concerned over the implications it would have on the future. But during this time, the sultan would receive yet more troubling news. In January 1186, the sultan's wife, Ismatadin Khatun, died. The plague in Damascus had reached her. This loss was especially severe for Salahuddin. In fact, he only received the news three months after her passing.

The sultan, now alone, sat miserably in his tent. Then Qadi Al-Fadil came from Damascus and arrived to see the sultan. He entered the tent of his ruler and dear friend, sealed the curtain at the entrance, and greeted him. He would remain by the sultan's side, as he suffered from his illness and the grief of the loss of his wife. Then Musa Ibn Maymun and Isa Al-Hakkari, Salahuddin's two best physicians, arrived with medicine for the sick sultan. The Jewish physician and his Muslim counterpart, whom the sultan had sent many times to those who needed their treatment, now were responsible for guarding the health of their leader. After they finished preparing the fluid, they gave it to him. Salahuddin drank from the cup and then immediately reclined on his bed to rest.

With the medicine beginning to pull him into a deep sleep, his dear friend, Al-Fadil, grabbed his hand and told him, "If Allah restores your health, nothing will thwart you from your path."

Chapter 16
The Horns

16th-century Turkish Cavalry Armor, The Louvre Abu Dhabi, UAE

The virtues of the Holy Land, Bilad Al-Sham, ran deep within the imagination of the early Muslims. Bayt Al-Maqdis, the city of Jerusalem, was itself a center of faith, which continued to inspire the Muslims in their struggles for years to come. It was recorded in a Hadith that the Prophet Muhammad ﷺ said to his followers: "A group of my Ummah will remain on the truth. They will vanquish their enemy, and those who oppose them will not be able to harm them until Allah commands."

The companions asked: "Where will they be, Messenger of Allah?" The Prophet ﷺ replied: "They will be in and around Bayt Al-Maqdis."

Immediately following Guy's coronation, Reynald de Châtillon was renamed the Lord of the Oultrejordain. With Kerak returned to him, he began preparing for war with the Muslims once again. Soldiers and knights passed in and out of its gates. And it was not long before the Templars returned. Gerard de Ridefort was appointed as the Grandmaster of the Knights Templar, effectively commanding full control over the order. Together, Reynald and Gerard immediately planned to strike deep into Ayyubid territory, aiming to raid south again into the Hejaz. One day, in the year 1187, before the sun had cast its light on the land, Gerard and Reynald gathered their horsemen to begin their raids.

With the kick of their heels to their steeds, Kerak's doors released its beasts of war. In the desert region of northern Arabia, caravans from Damascus were on the road to Medina and Mecca for Hajj. After riding on their camels for several hours, the caravans stopped to rest nearby wells and pray. When they halted in the tracks of their journey, across the dunes, Reynald and Gerard's Templars spotted them. The cavaliers of the Knights Templar had come from beyond the desert and charged with their swords drawn and their horses mad with a brutal momentum.

When it was all done, the desert had gone silent. Nothing, except for the cawing of the crows above, filled the air, a sight that had awaited the shock of the sultan's reconnaissance units. At the sultan's camp outside Damascus, he called for his operatives to bring him news of what had transpired in the Hejaz, along with retrieving his sister from one of the endangered caravans. He was already aware of the crime that had taken place on the Hajj routes, but with these revelations having finally come to light, it drove him at last to elect the path of war.

In Jerusalem, Guy once again held another assembly with his noblemen, his knights, and the Muslim messengers that had been sent from Damascus. Salahuddin's message was blunt: turn over to him the heads of those responsible for the raids and obey the sultan's order to completely surrender Jerusalem. These demands could not have been given to a worse audience. Every nobleman, bishop, baron, and knight preferred the king to elect war with the Muslims. For Guy, the message that he would send back to Damascus, was already decided upon. The envoys were removed from the king's court and dismissed.

The next day, outside the walls of Jerusalem, the knights of the Templars, led by their grandmaster, made the long ride by horse to the north of the kingdom. At the fields of Cresson, in the area surrounding Nazareth, the first outbreak of hostilities would take place. The Crusaders would meet an Ayyubid force under Gökbörü. And by the wells, Gökbörü and his Turkoman riders waited patiently, often stalking the Crusaders behind the hills. Gerard de Ridefort and Roger de Moulins, Grandmaster of the Knights Hospitaller, stood together to meet the Ayyubids head on. The Crusaders would advance forward, meeting the Turks in open battle on the field, but only for a brief moment.

Gökbörü then led his men away and began fleeing across the plain. The Templars pursued them, but as they did so, the organization of their battle formation began to fall into disorder. Noticing this, Gökbörü turned his men around and moved to attack this vulnerability. It was a feigned retreat and a disaster for Gerard, the Templars, and the Hospitallars. The Crusader army was defeated and left destroyed at Cresson. In and around Jerusalem, Guy had been preparing for war. The knights of the Latins, Ibelin, Tripoli, and Jerusalem all gathered outside the city. 20,000 men answered Guy's call, who along with his barons, gathered at the behest of this army's creation, but their plan of confrontation would change with the return of Gerard de Ridefort from the north of the country.

Days later, the Templar grandmaster returned to the king beaten and exhausted, informing him of the disastrous defeat of his army at the Cresson plain, the Muslim seizure of all the water sources around Tiberius, and the looming arrival of some 30,000 soldiers under the sultan himself. Accompanying the army of the Crusaders was the True Cross, a Byzantine relic which contained a piece of wood, believed to be a fragment of the cross of Christ. It was therefore the holiest relic in Christianity. Believing their army, blessed by the cross, to be impervious to defeat, the Crusader lords confidently met the sultan's challenge head on.

Once they were rallied into their respective contingents, the army of the Cross, in the blistering summer of 1187, marched north, into a hilly and elevated region that constituted the land between Nazareth and the city of Tiberius, on the Sea of Galilee. And there, Salahuddin and his 30,000 strong army waited. Overlooking the land ahead of them, they waited for their prey. It was here that the sultan received the Englishman that he harbored in his army.

While there are not a great many details on who exactly he was, Robert of St. Albans is thought to have originally been a member of the Knights Templar. Traveling all the way from England to the Holy Land, Robert had spent his entire life committed to the Crusader cause. But after hearing word of the true chivalry of the Muslims and their sultan, Robert became disillusioned with the Crusader ideology, defected, converted to Islam, and escaped to join the ranks of Salahuddin's army.

In a secret correspondence with the sultan's spies, Robert had been feeding them critical information on the Crusaders, where all of their castles were located, the number of soldiers, the number of knights, the days worth of food and water, how long they could withstand a siege, how long they could wage an open battle, and a list of other details that aided the sultan in planning for the war with his enemy. Thus upon arriving in the sultan's army, Salahuddin rewarded Robert's espionage by giving him command over a group of his soldiers.

Far out into the distance, the Crusader army could be seen marching towards the Muslim position under the heat of the July sun. The sultan's spies informed him that the Crusaders had passed the town of Saffuriya, the last human settlement in the area. The only aid that the Franks would have on the road ahead were now the wells. Thus Salahuddin ordered his commander, Gökbörü, to set out for the remaining wells and destroy them. Trees and any other vegetation were also to be burned. Salahuddin's strategy would leave the Crusaders with nothing left in the land to sustain them.

Along with Gökbörü commanding an entire battalion of his army, the sultan had returned his nephew, Taqieddin Umar, to his standard position, pairing him alongside a new commander, the sultan's son, Al-Afdal. Born in 1169, the year his father had been made vizier in Egypt, Al-Afdal had been raised and educated throughout his father's career. And in 1187, at just 18 years old, Salahuddin gave him command of his own battalion.

The assignment that he entrusted Al-Afdal with was the seizure of Tiberius, the city that belonged to Count Raymond III. It was to be laid to siege, and the Sea of Galilee, at the shores of which it was located, was to be placed under full Muslim control. The Crusaders were to have zero access to its water. In the distance, the Crusader army grew increasingly worried, as the land that they passed through gradually became drier and less hospitable. They found the wells ruined and any trees that remained burned to the ground. Nonetheless, the army was directed to continue their advance forward.

With most of the water under Ayyubid control and everything else either dried up or destroyed, the Crusaders had no choice but to abstain from scavenging on what remained and move on. Everything had turned against them. The men, who had become stricken with thirst, began showing signs of disobedience and desperation. Count Raymond of Tripoli, who had been riding with the army, finally broke his silence and confronted the king and his men. Speaking for the army's need of finding water, Raymond's arguments won, and Guy agreed.

The Crusaders then ceased their costly advance and stopped in the middle of the valley, which was surrounded by many high ridges and hills. At night, all around them, the Muslims closed in from every direction. On all sides, they arrived and proceeded to begin their work in the darkness. Under the directive of the sultan, the spies collected large amounts of wood and twig and burned them atop the high ridges, where the wind blew, carrying the smoke and ash with it. In the morning, the Crusaders woke and were greeted by that thick blow of smoke from their enemy, who surrounded them and stood watching from the high mountains. The ash made the air unbreathable. They suffered from coughing and dehydration, as they had gone without water for days. Salahuddin, who saw all of this unfold to his design, ordered his commanders to begin the first major attack.

By noon, half of the Muslim cavalry was dispatched under Taqieddin. 8,000 riders descended from the mountain together and raced for the enemy. This tidal wave of shock and awe plunged the Crusader camp into a state of panic, as they were overwhelmed and forced to defend themselves against such a massive threat. Most of the Ayyubid riders were Turkic horse-archers, a dynamic form of warfare, almost entirely foreign to the unprepared European knights.

But the havoc that those riders unleashed would be checked. The Italian troops, armed with kettle helmets and crossbows, took up their defensive positions and began firing at the horsemen. Their superior armor earned them the advantage in that confrontation. And so as they were coming under fire from the Italians, the Ayyubid cavalry charge was forced to retreat. However, after they left, a gap opened in Salahuddin's lines. Raymond, who had been protected by his Tripoli knights and panicked by the shock of the attack, decided to use the opportunity to flee and abandon his role in the Crusader army.

Despite the minor setback for Ayyubids, their overwhelming pressure on their adversary was enough to shatter their coherence and organization. Seeing the near breakdown of his army, Guy called to regroup them immediately. In frustration, he snatched his mount's harness and turned it north, riding in that direction. Later that night, and after losing hundreds of men, the Crusaders traveled to Guy's chosen place of refuge.

Located in front of two extinct volcano peaks, they stopped at a place known ominously as *the Horns of Hattin*. A few tents were pitched for their leaders, while the rest of the men were either on guard or asleep. In the shadows of the midnight darkness, the sultan's spies returned to work. This time, they would set fire to the bushes in the Crusader camp. They were lit aflame, and the wind blew their ash into the air. It quickly spread, moving to burn down the tents, deteriorating the situation in the camp at an unprecedented pace. With smoke and panic rising all around them, Guy, Gerard, and Reynald woke to a disturbing atmosphere.

At dawn, on the 4th of July, 1187, before the red sun had arisen over the horizon, Salahuddin concluded his Tahajjud and Fajr prayers, as he had done before every battle. Having prayed to God for victory, he readied himself for the final assault. He donned his helmet, and upon exiting his camp, he was greeted by the zeal of his men, calling for him to lead them to that victory. And so he climbed his horse and towered above them all. With the red light shining upon him, the sultan unsheathed his sword and held it high in the air. The steel radiated with the sun's light. With their devotion reaching its peak, Salahuddin knew that the time to unleash the fire of his war was then. He snatched his horse's harness and braced himself to ride into battle. He then pointed his sword out in the direction of the enemy and instructed his army to charge.

Inside the Crusader camp, Guy, Reynald, and Gerard were battling the first wave of attackers, defending themselves against the overwhelming storm of the camp. By the time they had dealt with the first wave, they witnessed the second one crash down upon them like a flood of fire. The sultan and his men led their cavaliers into the camp and slaughtered a great number of Crusaders, upon riding in. They swung and slashed their swords at their opponents and brought them to their knees.

Seeing the imminent collapse of the army and the potential capture of the king, the Templars, led by Gerard de Ridefort, concentrated their efforts around Guy de Lusignan, so as to protect their king. But in doing so, their army, already at its breaking point, suffered another loss. The True Cross, which the Crusaders brought with them into battle, was taken by the Muslims. This relic, existing in the Christian imagination, as the holiest object of their faith, was lost to the enemy. For the knights, it was a psychological blow. And with the loss of the cross, the army finally broke. The Templar grandmaster, Gerard de Ridefort, Reynald de Châtillon, and King Guy de Lusignan were all trapped, outmatched, and apprehended.

With the defeat of the Latins complete, the army of Salahuddin chanted in the heat of their victory, declaring, in a thunderous wave of a thousand voices, the cries of their great feat.

Salahuddin had won the Battle of Hattin. To his side, he saw Guy de Lusignan escorted by his Muslim captors, as a prisoner. Hundreds had been arrested in the aftermath of the battle. The sultan even caught sight of one Arab soldier, dragging behind him a throng of at least 20 Franks that he had captured himself.

Back up the mountain, where the sultan had pitched his tent, Salahuddin and his commanders all gathered together under the shade to conclude their victory. The sultan had with him a silver, gilded cup, which he filled with a scoop of ice from an iron box for cooling. He then offered it, as a gesture of respect, to Guy de Lusignan, a fellow king. He drank from it, but then passed it on to Reynald, who gladly drank all of it.

Salahuddin then told Guy, "It is you who has given him the drink. I give him no drink." Annoyed by the Frank's lack of any guilt, Salahuddin's patience with Reynald ran thinner than a thread of string, as his companions also awaited his inevitable decision to execute him for his crimes against the Muslims. He could have done it whenever he deemed it, however, his principles taught him of the importance of mercy, and so he offered it. Salahuddin gave Reynald one last chance: convert to Islam and his life would be spared. Reynald de Châillon refused. The sultan looked down subtly at his sword's hilt. He grasped it and then immediately drew it out. He slashed it across Reynald's neck and tore it open. Reynald then collapsed to his knees and was pulled away by two of the sultan's Mamluks. Guy's face swelled with fear that he would be next. Men the likes of Gökbörü and Taqieddin surrounded him like wolves, but their boundaries were already established by their sultan.

Out of the shade, in the hot sun, Reynald was restrained by his killers. The furious sultan then had Reynald decapitated. By the sultan's hand, the Crusader lord was dead. This act was the sultan's retribution for Reynald's numerous raids, particularly his attacks on Muslim caravans and his failed attempt to sack Mecca and Medina. Killing him was Salahuddin's act of justice. Having finished the deed, Salahuddin then returned to the tent, where Guy stood nervously still.

In a statement, reaffirming his commitment to chivalry, Salahuddin stepped towards Guy de Lusignan and promised, "It is not the custom of kings to kill kings. But that man had violated all bounds, therefore did I treat him thus."

Then he turned to his men and inquired about the rest of the battle's details. Gerard de Ridefort was held prisoner with the rest of the Templars. Following decades of battles and numerous confrontations across the Levant, the grandmaster of the Knights Templar had been captured and defeated. But from a place of political opportunism, the sultan would spare Gerard's life to use him as a bargaining chip.

As for the rest of the Templars, Salahuddin understood that these knights were zealots and were thus a threat that could never be dissuaded from taking up arms again. If he granted them their lives, his mercy would be abused by their malice, and they would return to open war with the Muslims once again. The sultan thus ordered that all of them be put to death. Their decapitated heads and piled corpses would mark the site that was the Horns of Hattin, the place that represented Salahuddin's tactical masterpiece and triumph over the disgraced Latin Crusaders.

With the battle won and nothing standing in his way, Salahuddin would set aside time during the final months of the summer to turn his army on the last Crusader holdouts. As soon as Hattin ended, he dispatched his armies to Acre, Haifa, Caesarea, Jaffa, Askalan, and Gaza. After securing the ports of the Mediterranean coast, all but Tyre, he cut off all means of reinforcements from Europe. And finally, he would make his march on the final objective of his great campaign, the city of Al-Quds, Jerusalem.

Chapter 17
The Opening

The Dome of the Rock at Masjid Al-Aqsa, Jerusalem, Palestine

"Glory to the One Who took His servant (Muhammad) by night from Masjid Al-Haram (Mecca) to Masjid Al-Aqsa (Jerusalem), whose surroundings We have blessed, so that We may show him some of Our signs. Indeed, He alone is the All-Hearing, the All-Seeing."

سُبْحَٰنَ ٱلَّذِىٓ أَسْرَىٰ بِعَبْدِهِۦ لَيْلًا مِّنَ ٱلْمَسْجِدِ ٱلْحَرَامِ إِلَى ٱلْمَسْجِدِ ٱلْأَقْصَا ٱلَّذِى بَٰرَكْنَا حَوْلَهُۥ لِنُرِيَهُۥ مِنْ ءَايَٰتِنَآ إِنَّهُۥ هُوَ ٱلسَّمِيعُ ٱلْبَصِيرُ

- Surah Al-Isra of the Quran (17:1)

On the 20th of September, the army would arrive outside the holy city. There they stood, surrounding it. As a result of his scorched-earth tactics in the countryside, the sultan flooded Jerusalem with refugees, impeding the livelihood of the city's populace. The annihilation of the king's army at Hattin had deprived Jerusalem of the knights needed to protect the city professionally. Outside the walls, the sultan and his commanders, flanked by the foundations of their army's siege weapons, towering overhead, gazed at the city's walls.

When the sun set over the land, he began the siege. His catapults and trebuchets fired at Jerusalem's defenses through the entire night, reducing large portions of them to rubble. And during the day, the Muslims sent boarding parties on their siege towers to scale the walls, but their attempts to storm the defenses were repulsed.

This cycle of destruction and violence continued for twelve days. And each day it persisted, the walls fell further and further into ruin, and the dead of the Franks multiplied. Then on the 2nd of October, on the day that the sultan planned to mount his largest offensive, he was informed by his commanders that the city's defenders had responded to his offer of capitulation. Escorted by his Mamluks, he met the commander of the city's garrison, Balian de Ibelin, in the scorched field between his army and the battered, crumbling walls of Jerusalem.

With the sultan and his army on the verge of conquering the holy city, fears arose, among the Crusaders, around the fate of their holy sites. To prevent the Church of the Holy Sepulcher from falling into the hands of the Saracens, the Crusaders allegedly threatened to take drastic measures, including utterly destroying the church. They had also threatened to demolish Al-Aqsa and every site in Jerusalem holy to the Muslims. If the Crusader endeavor came to an end and Jerusalem was lost once more, then the Latins would lay waste to all of it. They would have Jerusalem die along with them. Neither they nor the Muslims would have anything left to love in the holy city. However, the sultan would present them with a more preferable offer.

Salahuddin promised that he would grant anyone, who wished to leave, safe passage to the sea. The emigrants would pay their due fee, one which was low enough for them to afford, but the poor of the city could leave freely if they chose to. Those of Jerusalem, who were born upon its land and wished to stay, were given the freedom to stay under Muslim rule. None would be harmed. None would be forced from their homes. None would be forced to give up their religion.

Thus, it was under these terms that the Crusaders surrendered Jerusalem. Once the preparations and conditions were finally met, the Muslim army of Sultan Salahuddin Al-Ayyubi entered the city on the 2nd of October 1187, a day which coincided with the Islamic commemoration of Al-Isra wal-Mi'raj, the day when Prophet Muhammad ﷺ made the blessed journey to Jerusalem and the Heavens in one night. And it was that experience in early Islamic history that honored the Muslim Ummah with Al-Aqsa, where the Prophet ﷺ led the prophets before him in prayer towards their Lord, symbolizing the Muslim nation as the successor of all the monotheistic nations of the past.

For over 80 years, since the infamous massacre that marked the beginning of the Crusader presence in Jerusalem, there had not been a single prayer given at Masjid Al-Aqsa. And so as Salahuddin toured Jerusalem, for the first time in his life and likewise for every man in his army, the sultan understood very well what Jerusalem was and what it meant to the Ummah. This conquest was not like anything that came before, and it would not be like anything that would take place after it.

With the ideas flowing through his mind, of everything that Jerusalem meant to him and his faith, Salahuddin was reported to have said to the Latins that day, "Al-Quds is to us as it is to you. It is even more important for us, since it is the site of our Prophet's journey and the place where the people will be gathered on the Day of Judgement."

Entering on foot, the sultan walked with his companions through the stone streets as the ruler of the holy city, in a manner which attempted to replicate the humility of Omar Ibn Khattab (رضي الله عنه), the second caliph of Islam, who first conquered Al-Quds for the Muslims. The people of the city watched as he and his entourage made their way through the streets. And in keeping his promise, the sultan acted towards them with tolerance and mercy.

Just as the evils of history often repeat themselves, so too can the virtues. And on this day, Salahuddin's entrance into Jerusalem rhymes in many ways with the entrance of Prophet Muhammad ﷺ into Mecca. On that day, the Prophet ﷺ assured the people of Mecca, who had him and his followers harassed, persecuted, harmed, sworn at, and driven from their homes with such hatred and bigotry, that he would not do upon them, as they have done upon him. He forgave them.

And when Salahuddin entered Jerusalem, and the people wondered what the Saracens would do, he relieved them with his forgiveness. His mercy to the Christians of Jerusalem is what made his character so admired in the Western imagination. Because out of the perceived barbarism that was the Muslim world in Europe's eyes, here was a leader, who in his chivalry was exemplifying one of the most Christian virtues of them all: forgiveness. But, of course, Salahuddin did not learn these virtues from the West. He learned them from the Sunnah of the Prophet ﷺ.

Eventually, Salahuddin and the men beside him, Al-Adil, Qadi Al-Fadil, Imadeddin Al-Isfahani, Al-Afdal, Gökbörü, Taqieddin, and numerous others, arrived upon the grounds of Masjid Al-Aqsa. The final remnants of the Crusader occupation were dismantled. The cross that was raised over the Dome of the Rock was brought down. In the Qibli Mosque, where the headquarters of the Templars were erected, the Muslims found their banners. The sultan ordered for them to be pulled down and burned. With not a single Templar left in the city, their belongings, relics, and treasures were confiscated. And the operations of their citadel were utterly dismembered. 220,000 gold dinars were distributed amongst the soldiers of the Muslim army. Salahuddin took none of it for himself.

Inside the Qibli Mosque of Al-Aqsa, as renovations continued within the mosque's interior, Salahuddin and his men entered the prayer hall together. After installing the wooden minbar that Nureddin Zengi had commissioned to be built for the recapture of Al-Aqsa, Salahuddin's promise to his master, his army, and his nation had been fulfilled with the very presence of the returning Muslims on those grounds. On the first Friday of that week, once the masjid had been properly restored, the sultan and his men appeared before God once again on the sacred grounds of Bay Al-Maqdis. After Qadi Al-Fadil gave his sermon to the Muslims from the minbar, the prayer finally commenced with the sultan serving as the imam of the congregation. And just as he led them in battle, the sultan would lead them in prayer.

Salahuddin's liberation of Al-Quds, the holy city Of Jerusalem, in 1187, was not the end of the Crusades, but it was the beginning of the end. More armies and new kings would venture to the Holy Land to reclaim it for the Cross, but none would succeed in securing neither land nor the city for long. Al-Haram Al-Sharif, the Noble Sanctuary of Masjid Al-Aqsa, had always been at the spiritual heart of the Muslim world.

It was where the Prophet Muhammad ﷺ led the prophets in prayer, made the Night Journey to Heaven, and honored the Ummah of Islam. It was that honor that compelled the Muslims under Salahuddin to unite first as brothers, then as statesmen, and finally as armies in order to restore Al-Quds and return it to the rule of Islam. And for the next seven centuries, it would remain under Muslim rule. However, the struggle between East and West for control over the holy city would live on, even until the end of the reign of Salahuddin.

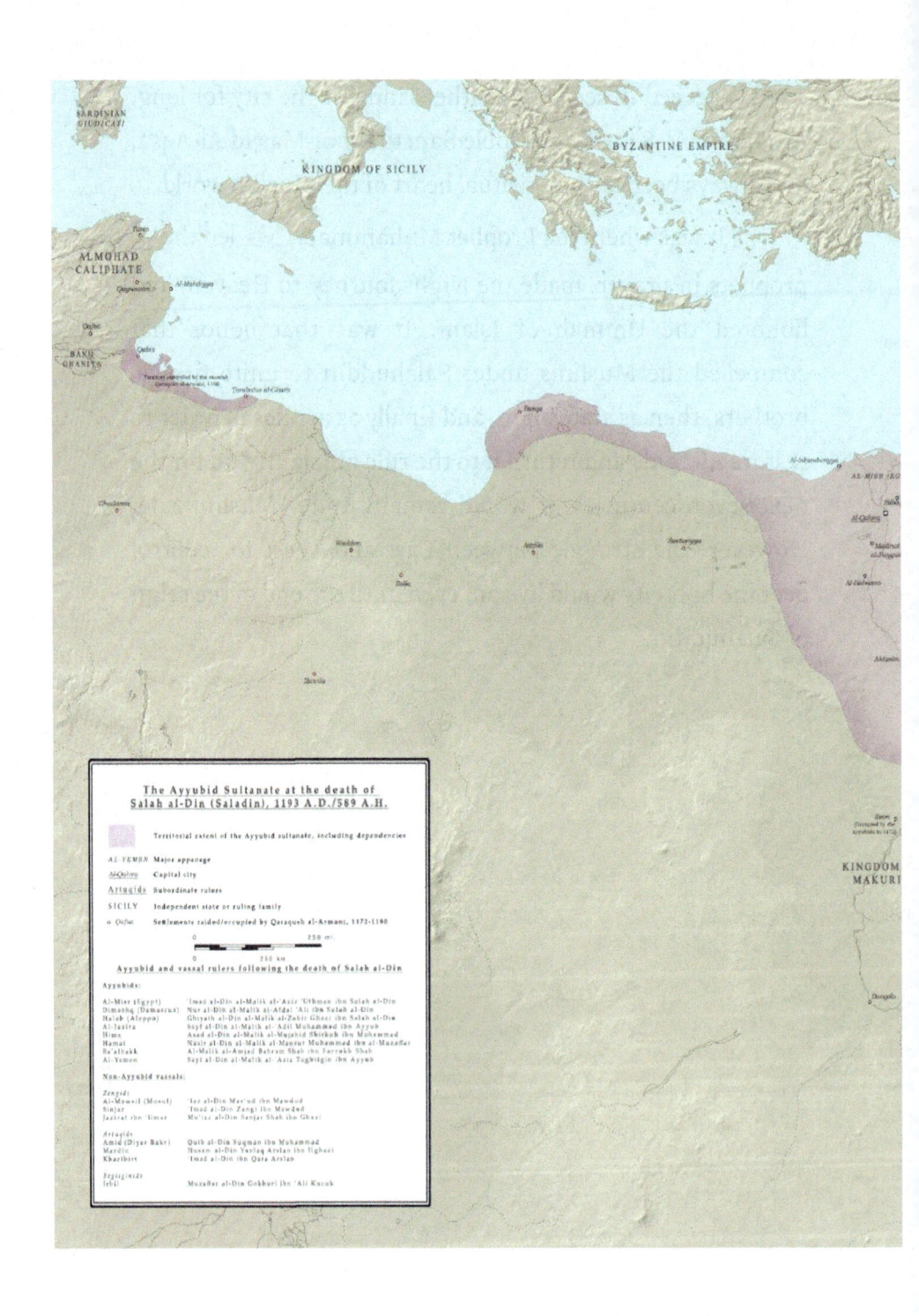

The Ayyubid Sultanate at the death of Salah al-Din (Saladin), 1193 A.D./589 A.H.

Territorial extent of the Ayyubid sultanate, including dependencies

AL-YEMEN   Major appanage
Al-Qahira   Capital city
Artuqids   Subordinate rulers
SICILY   Independent state or ruling family
○ Qafsa   Settlements raided/occupied by Qaraqush al-Armani, 1172-1190

Ayyubid and vassal rulers following the death of Salah al-Din

Ayyubids:

Al-Misr (Egypt)	'Imad al-Din al-Malik al-'Aziz 'Uthman ibn Salah al-Din
Dimashq (Damascus)	Nur al-Din al-Malik al-Afdal 'Ali ibn Salah al-Din
Halab (Aleppo)	Ghiyath al-Din al-Malik al-Zahir Ghazi ibn Salah al-Din
Al-Jazira	Sayf al-Din al-Malik al-'Adil Muhammad ibn Ayyub
Hims	Asad al-Din al-Malik al-Mujahid Shirkuh ibn Muhammad
Hamat	Nasir al-Din al-Malik al-Mansur Muhammad ibn al-Muzaffar
Ba'albakk	Al-Malik al-Amjad Bahram Shah ibn Farrukh Shah
Al-Yemen	Sayf al-Din al-Malik al-'Aziz Tughtigin ibn Ayyub

Non-Ayyubid vassals:

Zengids
Al-Mawsil (Mosul)	'Izz al-Din Mas'ud ibn Mawdud
Sinjar	'Imad al-Din Zangi ibn Mawdud
Jazirat ibn 'Umar	Mu'izz al-Din Sanjar Shah ibn Ghazi

Artuqids
Amid (Diyar Bakr)	Qutb al-Din Suqman ibn Muhammad
Mardin	Husam al-Din Yavlaq Arslan ibn Ilghazi
Kharibirt	'Imad al-Din ibn Qara Arslan

Begtiginids
Irbil	Muzaffar al-Din Gokburi ibn 'Ali Kucuk

Murad 152

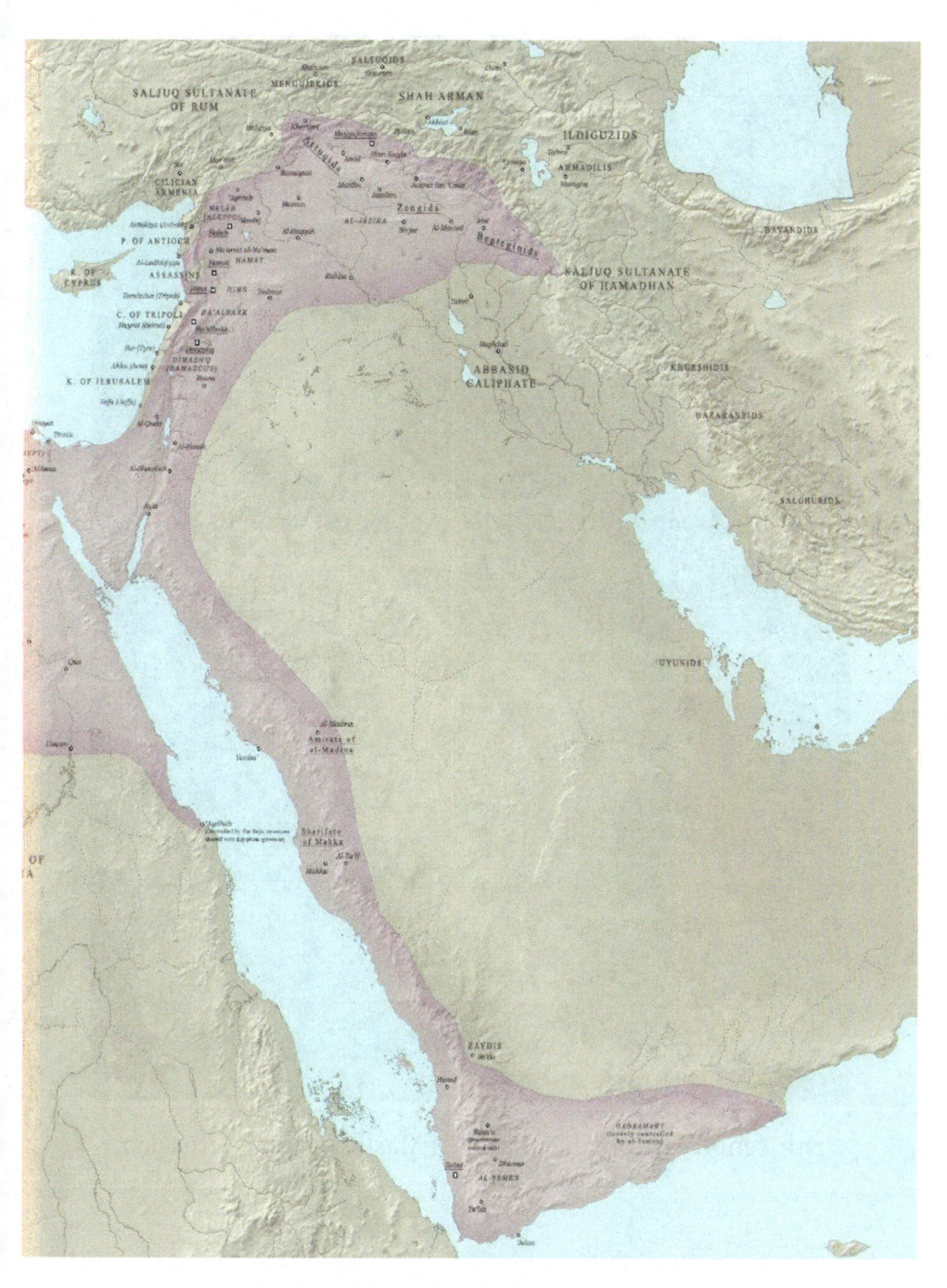

Map of Salahuddin's Dominion

Murad 153

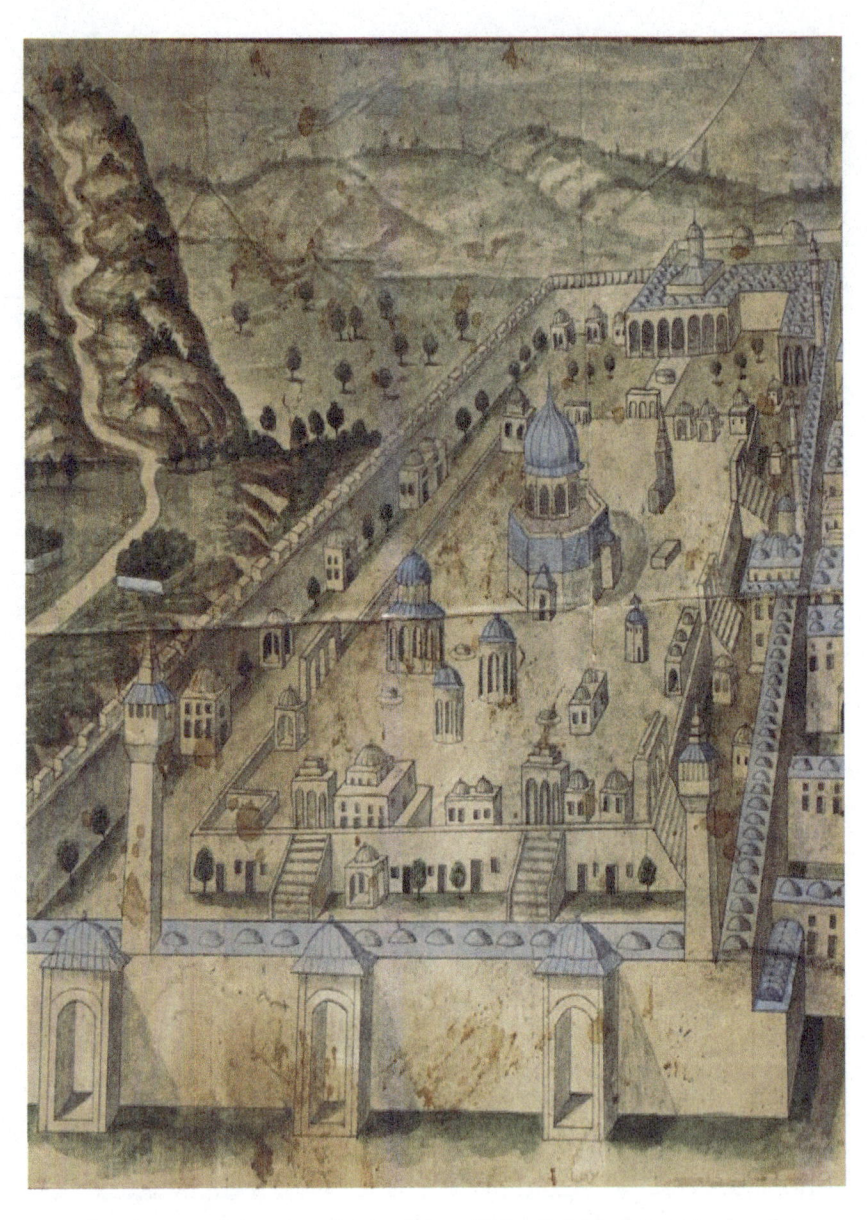

19th-century Ottoman Painting of Masjid Al-Aqsa, Jerusalem

Mosaics from the Umayyad Mosque, Damascus, Syria, depicting scenes from *Jannah*, "Paradise"

"Tree of Life" Mosaic from the Umayyad Palace of Qasr Hisham, Jericho, Palestine

Dome of the Mosque of Cordoba, Spain

Murad 156

Old City of Damascus Oil Painting

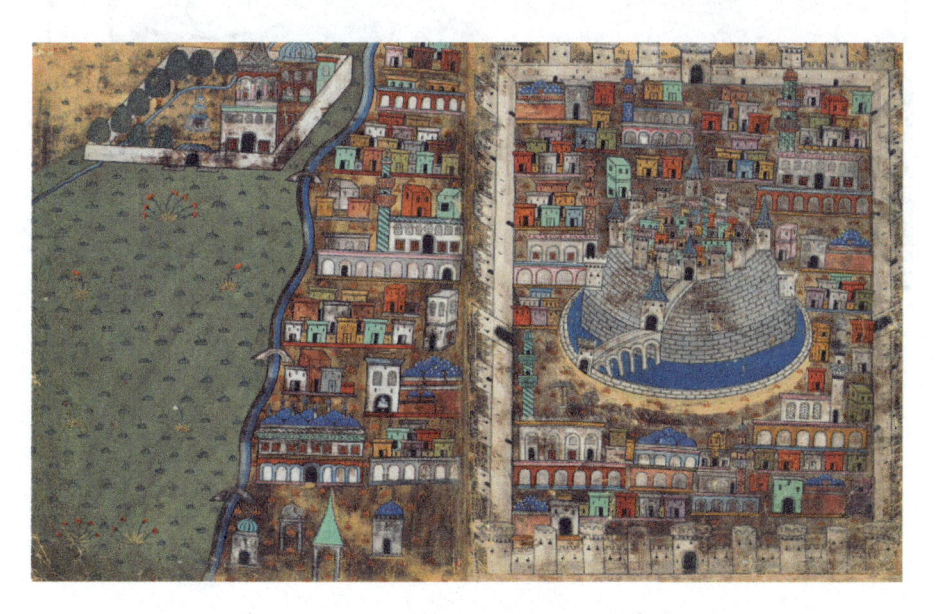

16th-century Ottoman Painting of Aleppo

Murad 157

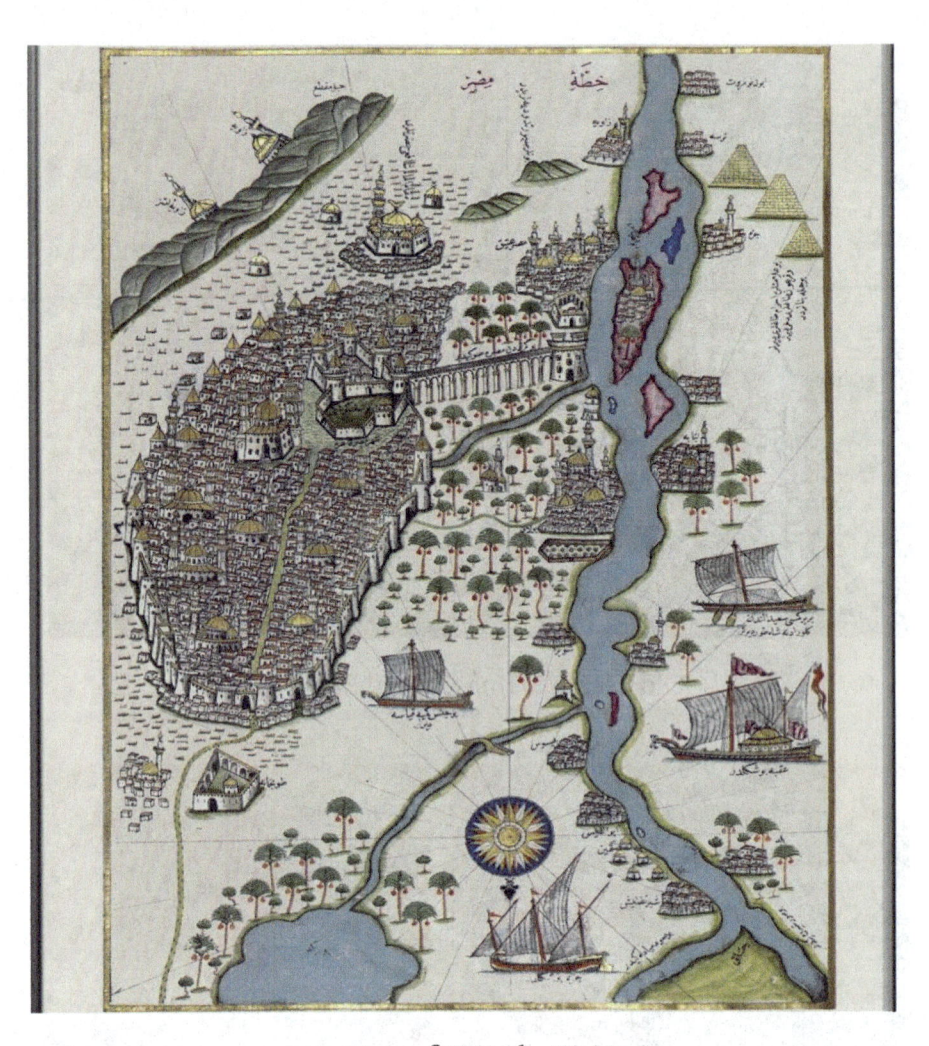

1555 Map of Cairo by Piri Reis

19th-century Ottoman Painting of Masjid An-Nabawi, Medina

19th-century Ottoman Painting of Mecca

Murad 159

1537 Ottoman Painting of Istanbul by Matrakçı Nasuh from

Istanbul University Library, Turkey

Murad 160

Part IV
The Siege
(1187 - 1191)

Statue of Salahuddin
Damascus, Syria

Chapter 18
The Victor's Burden

Dirham of Salahuddin (1190 - 1191)

The winter that marked the end of 1187 brought Europe the harsh cold and the shocking news. For almost an entire century, Europe had sent generations of knights, landowners, and kings to venture to the Holy Land. For 80 years, Palestine was the battleground of the Crusade, whose soil would become the burial grounds for thousands of Europe's elite families. Time and time again, men and their families would travel, settle, fight, profit, and die in the Holy Land.

And in 1187, a new wave of Crusaders would begin to gather around the cause for a new crusade to recover Jerusalem. News from across the Mediterranean would reach

Europe's monarchs. Pope Urban II, Holy Roman Emperor Frederick Barbarossa, and the French and English kings, Henry II and Philip II, all received the same message and the same shock. Barbarossa sat back on his throne, dwelling greatly on the news. The Pope's heart sank, and he supposedly died of a heart attack from his grief. The English and French kings too were greatly alarmed. In their castles in France, they reacted with outrage over Jerusalem's fall and the name of the man responsible for it—*Saladin*. And thus with that name spoken, which ran through the minds of the West with fury, the Third Crusade was born instantly.

In the Levant, from which his name arrived to the ears of Europe, Salahuddin had his armies outside the coastal seaport of Tyre, known in Arabic as *Sur*. The walls of the city were battered by the barrage of the besieging army's catapults, which launched numerous volleys of debris, over the course of multiple days, to break the resilient defenders of the city. The man in possession of Tyre was Conrad of Montferrat. This Crusader lord belonged to a noble house from northern Italy, producing many great Crusader leaders over its history, such as his relative, Boniface of Montferrat, who in later years, would participate in the Fourth Crusade against Constantinople.

Conrad had reached the Levant by way of Constantinople around the same time that Salahuddin launched his campaign against the Kingdom of Jerusalem, the campaign that witnessed Hattin and the reconquest of the holy city. With Conrad, as the governor of Tyre and adamant against surrender, Salahuddin called for a withdrawal. His army then returned to Damascus.

In the months following the Battle of Hattin, the sultan's administration had consolidated effective command over the territories possessed by the sultanate. The Levant was secure. Any remaining Crusader presence, whether in Tripoli, Antioch, or Tyre, could only growl in defiance to his conquest. Within his administration, Salahuddin appointed two more of his own family to high posts within his state.

His son, Az-Zahir Ghazi, had ruled Aleppo since 1186. When the province had been fully integrated into Salahuddin's state, Az-Zahir was made its official governor, in 1187, giving his status immense significance within the region. In Egypt, Salahuddin had assigned the entire province to another son, Al-Aziz Uthman. He assumed his role in the winter between 1187 and 1188. As for his eldest son, Al-Afdal, Salahuddin would reward him for his exemplary performance at Hattin with the governorship of Damascus itself. The city would be granted to him in 1189.

Having spent months besieging the remaining coastal cities of the Latin Crusaders, the sultan's campaign, which began with Hattin, had finally come to a close. The one city to have escaped his conquest was Tyre, whose defenders held out with a tenacious but waning resilience. Tripoli and Antioch also of course withstood the sultan's wrath, as he had not made serious efforts against them. The campaign also witnessed the sultan lay siege to many Crusader castles in the region, resulting in the delivery of Kerak and Montréal.

The fabled castle of Krak des Chevaliers withstood Salahuddin's siege. Built on a high mountain, 23 miles from Homs, the castle proved itself once more to be impregnable to the sultan's attempts. Its sheer altitude alone made the operation an incredibly daunting task. The Muslims withdrew, and Krak des Chevaliers remained standing for almost another century.

In Damascus, Salahuddin received Bahaddin Yusuf Ibn Shaddad as a visitor to the capital. Belonging to a family of Arab scholars from Mosul, Bahaddin had an extensive education in Islamic jurisprudence, hadith, literature, and the history of the Arabs. In his career, he became a respected scholar of the Shafi'i school of Islamic law, earning a reputation that brought his name to Salahuddin's attention. Upon completing his trip to Mecca to perform Hajj, Bahaddin later traveled to Damascus, where he would meet the sultan and join his circle of advisers. Along with Imadeddin Al-Isfahani, Salahuddin's vizier and prime minister, Bahaddin also served as a chronicler for the sultan. The first-hand accounts in his biography, as well as those written by Imadeddin, make both authors the two best primary sources on sultan of revival.

In the aftermath of Hattin and the reconquest of Jerusalem, Salahuddin would be advised by his growing inner circle on the state of affairs of the recaptured territories in the

Levant. From Tyre, Queen Sibylla of Jerusalem wrote a letter to the sultan's government, communicating to them her request for the release of her husband, Guy de Lusignan. Sibylla cited Guy's surrender of Askalan to Salahuddin and his overall cooperation with him since he was taken prisoner. She also expressed her desire to retire with him in Cyprus.

At this time, a number of Crusaders were ransomed by the sultan. Gerard de Ridefort was released with the involvement of his allies. The Templars conceded several key castles in the region, including Kerak and Montréal, sites which strategically bolstered Salahuddin's defense of the region. He also secured the release of many Muslim prisoners held by the Templars as well as a payment of 60,000 dinars for the release of the grandmaster himself. Upon Gerard's release, the sultan's spies would closely track his whereabouts. Believing Guy's leverage to be spent, Salahuddin agreed to release him. In Tartus, where Guy had been imprisoned, the former King of Jerusalem was given a horse and forced to swear an oath that he would never take up arms against Muslims again.

Chapter 19
The Gathering Storm

Coin of Richard I, Duke of Aquitaine (1172 - 1189)

In Europe, the call for the Crusade was heard across all corners of the continent. Throughout France, soldiers were armed, assembled, and sent on the march to the southern coast or to Italy. New taxes were imposed across England and France to finance the war effort in 1188. Leading this project was King Philip II Augustus of France and his vassal, King Richard I of England.

In 1189, Henry II, his father, died. In Westminster Abbey, on the 3rd of September, Richard was crowned, at the age of 32, as Richard I, King of England. His ascension over the crown also brought him into the ownership of the French possessions of his family, the House of Angevin, whose holdings encompassed lands in both the British Isles and the French mainland. They had grown considerably more powerful than the French themselves, but for the sake of peace, traditionally refrained from overstepping their limits of vassalage.

Unlike his father, Richard, however, would mold himself into an altogether very different king. The people of England would only witness his presence, in their country, for just a few months of his reign. While he was born in Oxford, he had actually spent most of his life growing up in France. The people of England barely knew him as their leader, but they would long remember him for the years of taxation that he levied upon the populace. The infamous Saladin tithe, which was introduced by his father, in 1188, was greatly increased under Richard's reign, collecting every pound and penny from the taxpayers to finance the Third Crusade.

Across the French and English countryside, their troops marched and grew in numbers. Every town on the road south, witnessed them pass and offered to them their sons to join their ranks. Eventually they reached their respective coasts. At the port cities of Europe, the fleets put together by the Venetians, Pisans, and Genoese were docked with many more ships still under construction. All vessels would sail for the Third Crusade, setting off on the journey to the Holy Land. Philip would depart from the port of

Marseilles, arriving in Sicily in March of 1190. Richard would also arrive in Sicily of that year, but he did so in April, sailing for the Levant much later than Philip.

In the lands thereof, Guy de Lusignan arrived before \ the city of Tripoli, entering it and being welcomed by the garrison there. In violation of his agreement with the sultan, Guy would then immediately make his trek to Tyre, crossing through the forested and hilly wilderness of southern Lebanon. Guy arrived outside the city and would demand to regain his lordship over it. However, Conrad of Montferrat would reject this demand from his supposed overlord, refusing to grant him the city. Guy had grown frustrated, for he would not settle on the sultan's forced plan for him to retire. He desired to regain his fallen kingdom. And now he would need to contend with a governor insubordinate to his rule.

Answering Guy's demand with a statement to inform him of his irrelevance, Conrad told the disgraced king, "I am only the lieutenant of the kings beyond the seas, and they have not authorized me to give the city up to you."

It was a setback, but it would not deter Guy. His desperation cemented him in his quest to regain his kingdom. He then turned his back to the city, climbed his horse, and prepared to leave with his bodyguards back to Tripoli.

Chapter 20
At the Walls of Acre

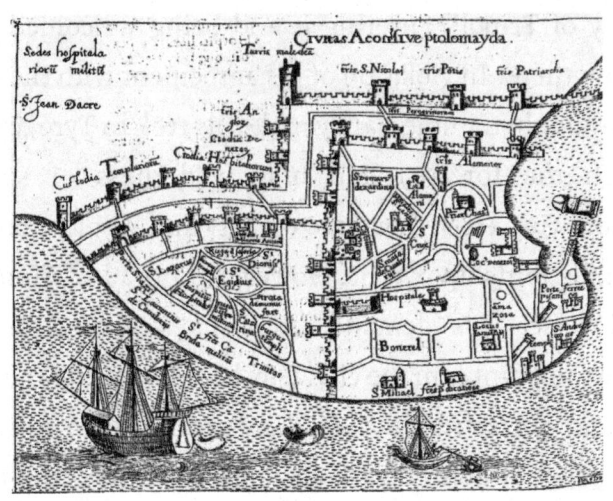

Map of Acre by Bosio, Giacomo, & Pierre de Boissat (1659)

In the spring of 1189, Guy de Lusignan regrouped with Gerard de Ridefort, the Templars, as well as his Pisan and Sicilian allies. After assembling a small force of knights and offshore vessels, Guy marched south with his men. Their destination was the city of Acre, known in Arabic as *Akka*, a high-risk target for them to even lay their eyes upon. On August 22nd, they traveled down the coastal Iskandaroun Pass, where they were spotted by the Muslims. The report was then delivered to Salahuddin in Damascus.

Acre, because of its proximity to Tyre, became an ever more strategic port, as the Third Crusade loomed closer. It enjoyed a geographically suitable location on the

Mediterranean. It sat on a peninsula, its sea walls were built atop high cliffs, and its land defenses stretched only half of a mile around the city, a perfect place for any defending army. Outside the city, the Muslim garrison spotted Guy's Crusaders outside the walls. They jeered and laughed at it mockingly, thinking them to be foolhardy to challenge them with such low numbers.

Guy and his men watched from afar. This time, they arrived with experience and a sense of strategy. They would do what Salahuddin did to them at Hattin: seize the high ground. Guy took the army to the top of Mount Toron. It was over a hundred feet high and gave him a strong, commanding view over Acre. It was his choice when the attack would be launched. Once he believed them to be ready, he issued his men the order. He would send them racing to the walls of Acre, climbing up with ladders and battling the Muslim defenders, taking them by surprise with shock and awe.

In Damascus, Salahuddin and his men agreed to embark forthwith at the behest of an army to crush this lingering Crusader threat. Atop the walls of the citadel of Damascus, the sultan lifted his helmet and placed it on his head with his visage this time expressing the look of an exhausted old man, tired from the years spent in war. He, together with his commanders, left for the courtyard, gathering their mounts and joining the army on the march to Acre.

As the hour of the Muslims' impending arrival drew ever closer, the Crusaders under Guy de Lusignan fought harder to take the city, constantly battling the defenders outside the walls, desperately trying to seek out a breach in the defenses. As Guy watched from afar with his men, his riders returned to him with critical news: Saladin was on the road. Guy ordered his army to withdraw from the walls and regroup at Mount Toron immediately.

Barely a mile in the distance, the sultan arrived with his men at the elevated plain of Al-Kharubba, where they had a view of Mount Toron and Acre behind it. As the soldiers pitched their tents for their leaders, Salahuddin remained on his horse and watched the enemy gather themselves against him. At Mount Toron, Guy and Gerard reorganized the army and descended from the mountain to face the Muslim army. Salahuddin saw this and learned of the numerical disadvantage that his outnumbered adversary now faced. A swift victory seemed inevitable, but he hesitated and opted only to maintain his defensive position on the high ground.

While the only commander he had initially brought with him was his son, Al-Afdal, many more commanders would soon arrive to join him. Gökbörü was the first to arrive, followed by Taqieddin. From across the empire, the sultan had brought a great many leaders to support him at Acre, such as Kotbeddin Zengi, the ruler of Diyarbakir and Hisn, Hossameddin Ibn Lajin, the ruler of Nablus, Seifeddin Ali Al-Mestub, the Kurdish chief of the Mehran and Hekkar tribes,

Mojahedin Berenkash, the fabled warrior of Sinjar, Zahiriddin Al-Hakkari, a cavalier and brother of Isa Al-Hakkari, the sultan's doctor, as well as the two veteran Mamluks of Shirkuh, Saifeddin Yazkoj and Arslan Bogha. Both of them remained by the sultan's side, as bodyguards for years ever since he ascended to lead Egypt, after his uncle's passing.

With the support of his commanders and soldiers beside him, Salahuddin initiated the first stages of his strategy. In the day, he sent his light cavalry to harass the Crusader camp. At night, he smuggled supplies and troops into Acre, among those men being Seifeddin Ali Al-Meshtub. He would join Governor Karakush inside Akka to defend and lead the city. This strategy of his, which he had employed many times in the past, would not avail him here. The single greatest element at Acre, that would ultimately undermine the tactics of the Muslims, was the Mediterranean coast.

From the horizon, European ships were seen sailing toward the beach. Every day, troops disembarked and trekked inland to join Guy's army. Within a week, 12,000 Frisian and Danish knights had arrived for the Third Crusade. Guy and his men stood watching in awe at the sight of the new Crusaders. After months of waiting, they had now come. Then from the hills in the north, Conrad of Montferrat entered the vicinity as well, bringing many thousands of knights and infantry with him. Guy and Conrad would meet on the northern side of Mount Toron before he had his troops join the ranks of Guy's army.

It was October 4th, 1189, and the first army of the Third Crusade had been assembled to meet the sultan. With the combined leadership of Guy de Lusignan, Gerard de Ridefort, and Conrad of Montferrat, they devised a plan for how to defeat the sultan's massive force. On the Acre plain, they chose to arrange their troops into three contingents. Rows of Frisian crossbowmen guarded the front, the Danish infantry took cover behind them, and cavalrymen were placed into two sections behind them all. Gerard's Templar knights were kept in the center, so as for him to have better control over the army's most elite units. The army began their march. They bid their time and energy, electing to approach their enemy at a walking pace. Salahuddin saw this and made his first move.

On the orders of his uncle, Taqieddin took off on his horse and left with his men, leading the lightly-armored cavalry across the plain. By late noon, they had made contact with the Crusaders. Taqieddin made a light skirmish and attacked with volleys of arrows. Upon meeting the weakened but furious Crusaders, who rushed up the hill to slay the Muslim riders, Taqieddin aimed to lure them away. And so he rode further east with his opponents in pursuit behind him. Back at the Ayyubid camp, the sultan saw this and believed that his commander was really retreating from the battle. He ordered the Mamluks to cover his right flank and sent a contingent to aid his nephew.

The Crusaders' march, at the moment, turned into a violent charge. They raced up the hill and fought Salahuddin's men, transforming the environment into one of clanging swords, battered shields, and fallen men. The Muslims were caught off guard and were being slaughtered in great numbers. Salahuddin, alarmed by this, was forced to abandon the front and the camp altogether. Within half an hour, the Muslims had abandoned the front and ran for the hills. The Crusaders seized the camp, where they looted and killed any stragglers. Even the sultan's camp was ransacked, where one of his servants was killed along with two of his guards, Ismail Al-Mokabbis and Ibn Rewaha. However, as the Crusaders pressed on, they did so at their own risk. Guy and Gerard raced ahead with the Templars, seeking to end Salahuddin at that very moment. But as the sultan retreated, his nephew returned with his men.

The sultan was furious. Taqieddin explained that some of his men had deserted in the chaos, only aggravating the sultan further. The camp was in enemy hands, and his army was on the verge of collapse. As the Crusaders drew near, the sultan would regroup his army and rally them to his side to face the enemy in battle. The sultan galloped in front of his soldiers, demoralized from the news of desertion so early in the battle. He would return a fiery rage to their hearts, inspiring them with an echoing speech, urging them not to yield. His men, as the frontline of the Ummah, were commanded to fight and, if necessary, die for the cause of guarding the Holy Land.

Soon the Templars had come into view and were about to deliver their final charge. But the long chase deprived their horses of their energy and momentum. Nevertheless, the Templars, at that moment, commenced their charge. With his enemies fast approaching, the sultan took the initiative. With his sword in hand, he kicked his stallion and sprinted for the Templars with his men following close behind him. Guy and Gerard, leading the Templars on horseback, met their Saracen enemies. The sultan and his Mamluks clashed and battled with the knights in the field. Gerard and his most hardened fighters plunged into the midst of the violence. However, by now, the Templars had gone too far and were without the support of the infantry that stayed behind, looting the sultan's camp.

As the Templars and their grandmaster persisted with resolve in battle, they had begun to suffer considerable losses, which would only multiply as the battle continued on. The sultan and his Mamluks began their slaughter of the Templars, whose force was quickly losing cohesion and was beginning to break down. By the hour's end, Salahuddin, together with his commanders and Mamluk bodyguards, succeeded in finally crushing the Templar assault. Their attack was reduced down to the very last man, leaving no survivors.

Hours later, after walking past the scattered corpses of the battlefield, Salahuddin discovered his old enemy. The grandmaster had been slain and killed in the heat of the action. In October of 1189, the bane of the Muslims, the spearhead of the Crusaders, the leader of the Knights Templar, Gerard de Ridefort, had finally died by the blade of Salahuddin's men.

Chapter 21
Bone and Iron

Statue of Emperor Frederick I Barbarossa, Goslar, Germany

After having crushed the Templar assault on the plains outside Akka, the sultan had trapped the surviving forces of Guy de Lusignan at Mount Toron, where the Crusader king fled to after the shocking defeat of the Templars and the death of its grandmaster. As he surveyed the deeds of his men, the littered corpses of the defeated knights, Salahuddin walked through the quiet battlefield. His men looked on with pride at the sight of their great leader, who had decisively led them to defeat the veteran Templar grandmaster. After receiving the praise and commendation from his men, he returned to his tent. He found it trashed by the Crusaders during the looting. As he reorganized his quarters, the sultan received Isa Al-Hakkari, his physician, a man he had known his entire adult life. The physician came with a distraught look on his face. His brother, one of the sultan's most capable soldiers, Zahirddin Al-Hakkari, was killed in battle. Moreover, one of his commanders, Emir Mojelli, had also been killed. With their deaths and the numerous other losses inflicted upon his army, Salahuddin would feel the pressure from his commanders mounting over him. Gökbörü, Al-Afdal, and Taqieddin all advocated for him to use their numerical advantage and ascend Mount Toron, storming it and annihilating Guy de Lusignan.

Salahuddin was adamant against such a decision. From his point of view, Guy's meager force was only a fraction of his adversary's total strength. His spies had informed him that Emperor Frederick Barbarossa had crossed from Europe into Anatolia. In light of such news, the sultan wrote to Emperor Isaac Angelos. Reaching a deal with him, the Roman emperor in Constantinople agreed to withdraw support for the Crusader army, which, by some realistic accounts, numbered a Herculean 100,000 men upon leaving Germany. The sultan also sent letters to Sultan Kilij Arslan II of the Seljuks. The Seljuk sultan assured Salahuddin that Anatolia would be guarded and that the Crusader advance would be put down. However, Salahuddin remained skeptical and did not trust him to be capable of defending his realm. And so he began preparations to recruit more soldiers and bolster his defenses in northern Syria.

As for the disorderly state of his army at Acre, the sultan would take resolute measures. He made it known to every soldier in his army that desertion, the likes of which was sustained on October 4th, would never be tolerated again. He issued orders specifically regarding the deserters that abandoned his nephew, Taqieddin, in the middle of the battle. He wanted all of them found and put to death.

As for the damages inflicted by the Crusaders, the sultan knew all too well that the army's disorganization remained unresolved. During the Crusader onslaught and the looting that followed, many belongings of the troops had been lost or displaced. The next day, in the morning, Salahuddin laid out everything in front of his tent, creating a sort of lost and found pile and allowing his men to collect their possessions upon swearing by Allah that it was indeed their property. This process ended on the 23rd of Sha'ban, as one of the clearest examples of the sultan's tradition of upholding fairness and looking after the interests of his men before his own.

Reforms were introduced as well to prevent that chaos that had occurred on October 4th. The army's baggage train of supplies and equipment was relocated to a position behind the main camp, on the fields of Al-Kharubba. The dead were also moved to a separate area there, so as to prevent the spread of disease within the army. On October 13th, the sultan summoned all of his commanders in his tent, where he would lay out a proposition to them. Salahuddin announced to them, "In the name of Allah, the Most Gracious, the Most Merciful, all praise be to Allah and peace and blessings upon the Messenger of Allah ﷺ, and his family, and his companions. As for what follows, the enemies of Allah and of our religion invaded our land and trampled the soil of Islam under their feet. However, already we see the inevitable triumph over them with which we shall overcome them, Insha Allah." "Insha Allah, Sultan," the council answered.

He would continue, "There remain but a small number of our enemies. I have come to the calculation that now is the time to utterly exterminate them. I take Allah to witness that this is our duty. We know that the reinforcements we are waiting for are those that my brother, Emir Al-Adil, is now bringing from Egypt. We also know the position of the enemy. If we leave them in peace, and they remain, they will continue to receive reinforcements from Europe. The opinion that I hold, and which seems to me as the best, is that we should strike them forthwith. We can end them in their camp. However, as I understand the risk of such an action, I will allow us to weigh our options together."

Upon the conclusion of the sultan's speech, the council became divided in opinion. Disagreements followed, and the sultan knew that he would not receive the support that he had hoped for to eliminate the Crusader threat once and for all. Ultimately, it was a mistake to seek out consensus from the war council, rather than for the sultan to wield more authoritarian leadership and make the decision to attack the enemy himself. It was eventually determined that the army would relocate back to Al-Kharubba, a safe distance from the Crusaders at Mount Toron, where the troops would have time to recover.

Many months later, in the late winter of 1190, Anatolia witnessed the arrival of the largest Crusader army ever put to the road. In the mountainous lands, ruled by the Sultanate of Rûm, the great European army of the Holy Roman Emperor marched confidently across the terrain. However, by this point, his army had dwindled from 100,000 to substantially smaller figures. Disease, desertions, and periodic ambushes by hostile Byzantines and Turks had inflicted considerable losses on the Kaiser's army. Arab writers, like Imadeddin Al-Isfahani and Bahaddin Ibn Shaddad, entered larger estimates into their records out of hysteria from the impending arrival of the most feared Crusaders. Nonetheless, the Holy Roman Emperor brought with him the single largest army among the other two Crusader kings, which European sources claimed to be roughly 30,000 at most by the time he set foot on the Asian continent.

Thousands of infantry and mounted knights accompanied him on the crusade, drawn up from across Europe. Decades earlier, Barbarossa was forced to quell a number of rebellions across his empire, and by 1188, he had imposed an unprecedented level of central authority over his feudal realm. In 1190, Europe's most powerful monarch, the red-bearded king, had set himself on a path of war against the Seljuk Turks. He had just defeated a group of ambushers on the Philomelion road, and continued his march through Anatolia, all the way to the heart of the Seljuks. Outside Konya, the capital of the sultanate, Sultan Kilij Arslan II had organized his army of beys and alps from across his domains, preparing them to grind down the assault that would soon come. He was prepared or so he believed. In the distance, the army of Crusader warriors emerged from the fog with their eyes set on Konya.

On May 17th, the German army had reached the city. The Seljuk sultan had mustered a significant number of troops for his defending army, but he would not rely on shere numbers alone. On the next day, when Barbarossa ordered his army to assault the walls of the Seljuk capital, Kilij Arslan left behind a small force of defenders to man the walls. Taking with him the vast majority of the army, the sultan rode out from the city with thousands of horse-archers and cavaliers. As the German army attacked Konya at the northern gate, Kilij Arslan led his men out of the southern gates, driving around the side of the city before they made contact with the Crusader army.

By now, Barbarossa had breached the walls, and his men began pouring into the city, looting and pillaging before the populace. The Seljuk defenders retreated towards the interior of the city to continue their defense from the citadel.

At this time, as Konya was being flooded with thousands of Crusaders, Sultan Kilij Arslan and his men had completed their flanking maneuver and attacked the Crusader army that waited outside the city from behind. The Crusaders were surrounded, and, after receiving serious losses, they were driven to the walls.

To save his army from total destruction, Barbarossa would enact a bold move. Leaving his men to continue the siege on the citadel, the Kaiser took charge of his struggling army, who were pinned to the walls, and led them forward in a brazen charge. With the fury of their horses and the advantage of their heavy battle armor, the Crusaders smashed into the Seljuk lines and severed their army in two. After suffering this catastrophic blow, the Turkish army disintegrated and retreated in all directions.

After completing his conquest of Konya, Barbarossa led his men to travel south near the Mediterranean coast. Passing through Armenian Cilicia, the Crusaders found themselves in friendly Christian territory, a relief compared to months of marching through hostile Byzantine or Seljuk territory, where they suffered from periodic skirmishes. Even though his army had fallen to 20,000 men by now, it was still leading far ahead of the other two Crusader armies of Richard I and Philip II, more than a match for Salahuddin. As they advanced eastward along the Taurus Mountains, the Kaiser set his sights on the land that awaited him next, Syria.

Chapter 22
Waves of Fire

The Shalandi, an 11th-century Arab Warship

In the Levant, winter had come. Its chill began to thaw, but persisted with one last storm at the end of 1189. The Ayyubid camp slept through it and tried to keep warm around their fires. Acre, however, was under the Latin naval blockade, and so they went hungry in the cold with dwindling food and supplies. One night, as Salahuddin planned and plotted in his tent, he was delivered poignant news. On December 20th, 1189, Isa Al-Hakkari, the sultan's doctor, teacher, and imam, passed away. His illness, caused likely by his asthma, worsened with the cold, and he died in his tent.

The sultan and his men performed the Janazah prayer and buried him. Salahuddin was deeply affected by this loss, and he grieved for days.

As for the Crusaders, their tenacity prevailed over their hunger. While the enemy camp rested, and their morale plummeted, the Franks dug massive ditches and trenches to protect themselves from any Muslim assaults and to further isolate Acre from receiving outside support. These defenses ran from the edge of Mount Toron northwards, until they made a sharp turn and continued west until they reached the sea, encircling most of the city. They also dammed the Na'mein River, known to the Latins as the *Belus River* from the Bible, which was diverted away from Acre, thus severely impacting its supply of clean water.

In fact, the situation in the city had become so dire that the garrison even offered terms of surrender to the Crusader camp. This proposition was soundly rejected, as the Franks believed that they would courageously conquer Akka through strength and the glory of battle. The Franks had also constructed larger siege weapons to use in their planned bombardment of the walls. Salahuddin had made a fatal mistake to postpone his offensive on the Crusaders, and now, there was no feasible way to dislodge them from Akka. The Crusader camp also received new arrivals to support the efforts of Guy de Lusignan. Humphrey of Toron, a young Frankish nobleman, had come from Tyre to join the Crusader king, to whom his family had given their loyalty since the time of Guy's ascendancy to the throne.

But in the early months of 1190, the Crusaders would be dealt a serious blow by the sultan. Salahuddin's Egyptian fleet had traversed the waves of the Mediterranean and reached the vicinity of Akka. 50 galleys from Alexandria, sent by his brother, Al-Adil, had broken through the Crusader blockade and delivered aid to the city. From a nearby hill by the beach, Salahuddin and his men watched, their faces gleaming with pride at the sight of their triumph, as they managed to finally break the blockade and deliver supplies to the city. The sultan's victory, in sinking the Crusader blockade and supplying the city with much needed food and equipment, raised the morale of the Muslims and ended any fears that Akka would be made to die off in the winter. For the first time in months, the city was supplied.

As the spring of 1190 began to gradually arrive, in the Crusader camp, Guy de Lusignan had convened with Conrad of Montferrat. The two rivals reached an agreement, wherein Conrad would be given rulership over Tyre as well as Beirut and Sidon. In exchange, Conrad would lend Guy the support of his vessels against the sultan. When the sun was about to rise and the night drew to an end, Crusader naval reinforcements entered the waters of Acre's vicinity. The fleet was a mix of Conrad's personal vessels, ships from the Sicilians, and those borrowed from the Romans.

On the northern hill by the coast, Salahuddin watched with his men the battle that would ensue. The Crusaders did so as well, but from the safe defenses of their camp. As the sun peeked over the horizon and illuminated the sky with its orange light, the two fleets prepared for the engagement. The Muslim fleet, more than a match for that of the Crusaders, sortied into a straight line. Their opponents, however, organized themselves into a V-shaped formation with their flanks extending ahead.

With the sounding of horns from the Latins and the beating of drums from the Saracens, the battle at sea began. They sailed towards each other and began firing arrows. Soon the flanks of the Muslim fleet were encircled by the Crusader ships, who used the advantage of their V-formation. Back on land, the Muslims watched intently. The sultan began whispering to himself prayers, reciting them quietly as he gazed out towards the water. Out at sea, the battle intensified. Projectiles and volleys of arrows were launched amongst the warring ships. Both the Latins and Muslims suffered heavy losses, but neither side gave up. Once they were close enough, the Crusaders boarded some of the Muslim vessels, leading to bloody battles on the decks. After repelling them, the Muslims tossed grappling hooks and threw planks onto their enemy ships, climbing onto their galleys in retaliation.

Soon, when the tide turned against them, the Muslims resorted to using Greek fire, a medieval version of napalm, which adhered to whatever it touched and burned for hours on end. This, however, backfired on the Muslims, who also suffered the loss of their own ships to the Greek fire. On both sides, sailors suffered gruesome fates and perished. But in the end, more Muslim ships had been sunk or driven away, leading to a victory at sea for the battered but surviving Crusaders. Akka was once again blockaded, and Salahuddin despaired, returning to his tent in disappointment. Later that day, in the late afternoon, before the sultan prepared to conclude the day, he received a letter from a servant of his. It was from his son, Az-Zaher, in Aleppo. The sultan learned of the news that Barbarossa had defeated the Seljuks and stormed Konya. It was clear that Syria would be next.

Fears in the Muslim army were growing, as the arrival of Barbarossa's army loomed over the region. In the sultan's camp and across Syria, the emperor's march sent shudders of fear into the hearts of the people. The sultan would once again assemble his council, where he elected to send the majority of them north, to Aleppo, Edessa, Samsat, Harran, and other cities for the defense of northern Syria. Even Taqieddin and Al-Afdal were sent north, while Gökbörü remained at his side at Acre. He also sent Bahaddin Ibn Shaddad, first to Damascus, where he would issue several letters, calling for reinforcements to be diverted to the north. But news of Barbarossa's fate had not yet reached Salahuddin or his allies.

In southern Anatolia, the Holy Roman Emperor marched onwards with his triumphant army. It was the summer of 1190. He had just beaten the sultan of the Seljuk Turks and taken his capital city, Konya. But he wasted no time and returned to the road for the Holy Land. They eventually made it to the Saleph River, where they were supposed to cross according to the information given by their Armenian guide. Growing frustrated with the slow marching progress of the army, the impatient Kaiser elected to make a fateful decision. He decided to cross the river himself.

He forced his horse to make the swim and commanded it to trek through the current. Midway, it lost its footing and threw the emperor into the water. He struggled to swim and shouted to his men for help. The heavy armor made it difficult for him to float. After struggling back to the surface for the last time and with his knights too far behind in the rough current, the emperor lost his energy and drowned. The mightiest European monarch to take the Cross was dead, and when he was brought ashore by his soldiers, all of them would foresee the disaster that would beset them. While his body was recovered, the crusade of Barbarossa drowned in that river along with him. Afflicted by disease and desertion, his army soon disintegrated and would never reach the Holy Land.

Far away in Damascus, the sultan instructed his scribe, Bahaddin Ibn Shaddad, to write another decree for the war effort. From the capital, he drafted the order and had it published for all cities across the state, from Aleppo, to Mosul, Jerusalem, and Cairo. Then he would travel to

Baghdad to gain an audience with the Abbasid caliph, representing Salahuddin as his diplomat and delivering a message that stressed the need for a united front against such a clear threat to the Ummah. Within days, the state had more soldiers drawn up and sent on the march to join the sultan outside Akka.

Chapter 23
Besieged

Siege Towers, Cassell's Illustrated Universal History, 1883

In Salahuddin's camp, more troops began arriving in the thousands. The sultan, now experiencing symptoms of illness, still refused to storm enemy lines. He maintained his defensive position and even sent his newly arrived reinforcements north to Syria, hoping to bolster Aleppo's defenses against Emperor Barbarossa, whom the sultan still had not learned perished. Fighting continued all throughout the rest of 1190 with no clear result emerging from either side. The Crusaders had filled the moat at the walls of Acre, but came under fire from the defenders. Nonetheless, the moat was filled, undermining the city's defenses.

Inside the head tent of the Ayyubid camp, the sultan assessed the state of the war with his advisers and commanders. As they studied the map before them, they concluded that Acre was completely surrounded by the Crusader siege, on both land and sea. To trouble the commander and their sultan even further, the spies delivered news from the Crusader camp, reporting on the atmosphere of high morale amongst the knights, as they awaited the arrival of Richard I and Philip II from Europe.

The spies also suspected an imminent assault upon Acre's walls. The siege towers would not remain idle in their position for long. Fearing that the besiegers intended to lay waste to Acre, following the rejection of the city's capitulation, Salahuddin and his commanders understood that action needed to be taken against the Crusaders to relieve Acre. For the sultan, his pressures were two-fold. Firstly, he needed to assault the Crusader camp to draw them away from the walls. And secondly, their siege towers needed to be eliminated. For this second objective, the sultan's commanders recommended a young man named Ali, an engineer and metal worker from Damascus, who concocted a volatile recipe of Greek fire that could incinerate the towers. The sultan promptly employed the young man's skills and involved it as part of his strategy.

It was the summer of 1190. The sultan and his army stood ready to fight on the plains of Al-Kharubba. Down the hill were the Crusader forces of Guy de Lusignan and Conrad of Montferrat, waiting for the battle to be called. Unbeknownst to any of them, further south, the sultan's men were dispatched. The sultan's spies smuggled Ali into Akka's walls. They waded through the swamp and under the cover of the fog of the early morning. On the northern hills, the Crusaders stood before the weakened walls, preparing for the attack. It had all gone quiet on the eastern front, until the sultan made his move. The sultan led his warriors to the bottom of the hill to face the Franks, who blew their trumpets and met them in battle. They clashed fiercely against each other, and the violence quickly ensued. Templar, Latin, Hospitaller, and numerous other orders of knights ruthlessly fought the Ayyubid infantry, while also boldly attacking the Mamluk cavalry, who struggled to repel them.

On the other side of the battlefield, the spies arrived with the engineer outside the city through the thick marshlands to the south. They passed through a well-hidden entrance to the cisterns that led into the city. Waiting for them were the defenders, who were relieved upon finding them. After being brought to the walls, Ali helped the defenders prepare the Greek fire. The sultan had smuggled with him into the city all of the materials that he had requested. He boiled them in naphtha, encased them in copper pots, each lit with a match, and then tightly sealed them in destructible jars, almost like a Medieval hand grenade.

In the Crusader camp, they began loading their siege towers and initiated the creeping march towards the walls. In the eastern hills, Guy anticipated the towers to attack soon, as he and his men could see them inching closer towards the land walls. The plans of both Salahuddin and the Crusaders depended on what happened at Acre's fortifications. Once the towers came into close enough range, the defenders seized their chance.

Rising from behind their defenses, they tossed and threw several jars of Ali's Greek fire at the towers. The flame latched itself onto the vulnerabilities of the massive structures and burned them. The machines quickly caught on fire. All three towers were lit ablaze and fell crumbling to the ground before the walls of Akka. The garrison celebrated in relief. In the Muslim camp, the sultan's son, Az-Zaher, arrived from Aleppo in time to witness the destruction of the towers. From the plains to the northern hills, all combatants had their eyes on the sight that was lit ablaze before them. Salahuddin eventually withdrew his men from the engagement, as his objective in destroying the towers was achieved.

But that day, simmering anger and frustration boiled in the Crusader camp. The knights urged that they sally out and fight the Saracens. Guy gave in to these demands. They left the defenses of the ditch and trekked back up the hills to meet the Muslims at their camp. Fighting quickly began and the Ayyubids were driven back, allowing the Crusaders to enter the camp. Once again, looting distracted them, and their ranks became disorganized, as they dispersed throughout the area.

This time learning from their past mistakes from October 4th, the sultan and his men immediately emerged with the Mamluks on horseback, rallying them together and charging against the plundering Crusaders. Guy's men were unprepared, and their disorder became their undoing. The Muslims charged into their ranks, killed thousands, and utterly devastated their army, sending them into a retreat. They later threw their corpses into the river to the south. The Crusaders, suffering a humiliating defeat, returned to their camp at Mount Toron, refusing to engage the sultan for months.

In the Muslim camp, where the damage had been mitigated due to the swift efforts of the sultan and his men, Salahuddin hosted his sons outside his tent, where he addressed, advised, and made dua for their protection. He emotionally embraced Az-Zaher, Al-Afdal, and Taqieddin before sending them on their journey back to the northern front. In the province of Aleppo, the sultan had sent them once again to defend the territory against the incoming Crusaders. Az-Zaher Ghazi, Al-Afdal, and Taqieddin concentrated their forces to engage waves of incoming German Crusader contingents, passing through southern Anatolia.

They had not yet learned of the death of Fredrick Barbarossa and of the condition of his now divided and disorganized army. However, the truth would soon be revealed to the sultan's men. As-Zaher would remain in the north for the entire duration of the war from that point onward, never again meeting his father. Taqieddin would depart from the northern front and return to the sultan at Akka shortly thereafter with the news that the Kaiser was dead and that the threat, once posed by his army, died with him.

In November of 1190, Salahuddin sent most of his exhausted troops away, back to their homes for the winter of that year. They had grown tired and stressed by the painful, year-long siege. The sultan gave in to their demands and allowed them their due time to rest in their period of dismissal. Taqieddin soon arrived, but came with plans to return to Hama. Seeing the state of the sultan's difficult position and the sickly state of his health, both he and Gökbörü elected to postpone their departures until after the winter had passed. Together they would stay to watch over Akka through the winter, which was a particularly cold one. Famine broke out in the city and in the Crusader and Muslim camps. The dwindling food and supplies worsened conditions greatly. Scurvy and trenchmouth were reported in Guy's army and in Akka, halting any fighting that could have taken place in the winter of 1190.

With the arrival of more suitable weather in 1191, the

prospects for the Crusaders improved. Guy and his men, as they walked in their camp, looked out to the sea and spotted Christian vessels preparing to make landfall. In April of that year, the French fleet, under King Philip II Augustus, arrived at the shores of the Holy Land. Guy de Lusignan would welcome the King of France, but was aware and unsettled by the close relationship between him and Conrad of Montferrat, due to bonds of family ties and of political allegiance back in Europe. Conrad was in fact the brother of Philip II's brother-in-law, creating, from Guy's perspective, an unsettling layer of proximity between his rival and the newly arrived king.

With the delivery of his ships from France, King Philip would instruct his crewmen to begin unloading massive disassembled structures, which were to be constructed into siege engines. Days later, once these weapons were made operational, the French began their bombardment of Acre, launching debris at the city's defenses on the northern side. Salahuddin watched from his camp. Once again, his inaction only prolonged the ordeal and worsened his chances of freeing Akka from the siege.

Chapter 24
The Fall

Penny of Richard I (1189 - 1199)

Several miles away, the last of the Crusader kings had finally made his debut in the region. Richard the Lionheart had arrived in Byzantine-held Cyprus, capturing the island for the Crusaders in June. Money and resources from the island had been secured for the Crusade, and they would be promptly sent to Acre, while Richard rested with his men in Cyprus. As his ships were docked and Richard stood on his vessel, overlooking the waves of the Mediterranean Sea, he was delivered a message from Guy de Lusignan. He called for the king's aid against the Saracens at Acre but also against Conrad of Montferrat. Guy had grown too fearful of Conrad's growing influence and sought external help. He had not forgotten his betrayal at the gates of Tyre.

For Richard, already seeing the signs of division within the Crusader camp was concerning, especially in the midst of the siege and before he even disembarked upon the Holy Land. In a matter of weeks, on the high waves of Acre's waters, his fleet appeared from beyond the horizon. The flag hoisted onto the mast was the Cross of St. George. Richard the Lionheart, the King of England, had announced to those on land that he had arrived. Aboard his galleon, he walked to the edge of the deck to set his sights on the city. Acre was already surrounded, but its defenders continued to hold their ground. Richard decided to land on the northern shores and disembark there. The boats bearing the flag of the English continued steadily, until land came within range and they disembarked upon the shore. Richard set boots on the soil of the Holy Land, as did his men for the first time in their lives.

He took an excursion and trekked the hills with his men, until they triumphantly arrived at the Crusader encampment outside Acre. Lined up and waiting to greet him, the Crusaders welcomed Richard, as he entered on foot. His arrival alone was an achievement in and of itself, for the sight of one of the greatest Christian kings to set his boots on the soil of the Levant, instantly raised the morale of the troops. The King of England would be introduced to the various Crusader lords, who would soon become his closest allies in the years to come. Henry of Champagne, Humphrey of Toron, Hospitaller Grandmaster Garnier de Nablus, Hugh of Burgundy, Conrad of Montferrat, and of course Guy de Lusignan all met personally with Richard.

Guy de Lusignan would grow especially close to Richard, as he was in fact a vassal to the English king, through his holdings in Angevin-ruled France. From the moment he disembarked from his ship, Richard the Lionheart had earned the loyalty of Guy's Crusaders. With his presence, the entire nature of the war had been transformed. Acre was trapped by land and sea, the northern hills were completely abandoned to the newly arrived Crusader armies, and the Muslims were now totally cut off from the city. However, in this time of rising tensions, Richard would engage with Salahuddin in a private correspondence of letters. In his tent, the sultan received one of these messages. Richard had requested to meet him in person, a face to face meeting.

Writing his own letter in return, Salahuddin responded, "It is not customary for kings to meet, unless they have entered into a treaty. For once they have spoken together and exchanged signs of mutual assurance, it would not be right for them to make war upon one another."

The letter was sent, and thus Richard's request for a meeting with the sultan was rejected. As the Crusader army remained encamped outside Acre, Salahuddin knew that, with each passing day, they had grown stronger in their entrenched position. But the Crusaders had one vulnerability: their division. Guy and Conrad continued a quiet war against one another, each being backed by one of the European monarchs. Conrad, a relative of Philip through familial marriage, was naturally supported by the French king. Because of Guy's jeopardizing of the kingdom's security and the resulting disgrace at Hattin, many of the nobles sought to enthrone Conrad to succeed Guy as the future king. Guy, a vassal of Richard through his holdings in France, received the support of the English monarch. These divisions would simmer, but would not become a serious detriment until after 1191.

Richard and Philip would waste no further time in pressing the siege on Acre. The Lionheart had sent his forces to the northern walls of the city. Philip joined Guy's Frankish army at the defenses by Mount Toron. Both armies bombarded the city together. Mangonels and trebuchets battered the walls once again and further weakened the ramparts of Akka. The Crusader kings watched, as the defenders struggled to withstand these heavy attacks. On Richard's side, an entire section of the wall had come down in a heap of debris. At that moment, the Lionheart pursued this chance.

The English made for the walls and took action. Despite his sickness, Richard took part in the battle by means of his crossbow, eliminating a few of the Muslim defenders at the ramparts, picking them off, as his men launched their own volleys of arrows. On the eastern side, Guy and Philip sent their troops. The soldiers chanted and swore that they would die in this last attempt to conquer Acre. They attacked

Acre's walls and brazenly attempted to breach them, swarming past the defenses. One prominent knight, a marshal from France, swore to an oath that he would fight to the death for the sake of conquering the city. He kept his promise and was killed at the walls. After his death, the Franks were routed and sent back. Richard's men also withdrew, as no significant breakthrough was made.

Nonetheless, the defense of Akka was completely exhausted with no hope of victory. The Acre garrison was on the verge of collapse, and the walls were so damaged that they had become unsafe to man. The battle was over. Salahuddin and his commanders returned to their camp, infuriated that after all they had done, all the years spent outside the walls of that city, it had become impossible to break the siege. The sultan looked back at the city, which was surrounded on all sides by the banners of the Cross. His eyes were wet with tears and his face reddened with anger. The nearly two-year-long battle for Acre ended in July of 1191, as a victory for the Crusaders.

Chapter 25
Massacre

Dirham of Salahuddin (1182 - 1183)

Throughout the entire first week of July, both sides entered discussions to secure the surrender of the city. Salahuddin was first to request terms of surrender, writing to the Franks that he would concede the city of Acre, along with all of its contents. He would also provide the return of holy relics to Christianity, such as the True Cross, followed by a payment of 200,000 dinars. However, these terms, as outlined by the sultan, were dependent upon the obligation of the Crusaders to spare the Muslim population of the city, to allow them their safe passage from its walls, and to guarantee the release of 1,500 prisoners. The message, prepared by his scribes, would be promptly sent to the Crusader camp.

As the sultan waited, he was delivered another message, this time from Aleppo with the return of his son, Al-Afdal. Salahuddin was informed of the news that Emperor Frederick I Barbarossa was indeed dead, how he drowned crossing the river in Cilicia, and how his army virtually disintegrated as it reached the borders of Syria. While this may have come as positive news to the sultan, as now the prospects of a two-front war had disappeared, it also came with the realization that he had sent all those thousands of men to reinforce Syria for nothing.

On July 12th, 1191, the deal was reached. The Siege of Acre, which lasted for two years, finally came to an end. Outside the city's demolished walls, Richard the Lionheart, Philip II Augustus, Guy de Lusignan, Conrad of Montferrat, and all their knights and soldiers stood in the hot sun of the Mediterranean summer. A mile away, Salahuddin and his army stood on their hill, overlooking the plain surrounding the city. That was the day Acre surrendered. It could have been worse, such as how the Crusaders planned for it to be, but both sides, exhausted as they were, had agreed to a carefully constructed deal, which ended the violence, rather than allowing for a bloody storm of the city.

The Muslim garrison evacuated from their defenses. From the gates, they all emerged, escorted by the Latin knights. While some watched in amusement at the sight of their defeat, Richard was actually impressed by the honor and admirable demeanor of the garrison, even in defeat. The

Crusaders too faced equally brutal odds, meeting them with undying resilience and tenacity. Cold winters, scorching summers, disease, hunger, and constant fighting had tormented them for two years. Hundreds of nobles, thousands of knights, and one grandmaster had perished. But in the end, they had won, and it was well deserved in their own right. The Crusaders had finally secured their port city, which they would use for the march on the rest of Palestine and Jerusalem itself.

As for the Muslims, their morale had been crushed. Salahuddin's reputation as the hero of the Muslim world had been shattered in a devastating blow. The Siege of Acre was the first time that he had ever been defeated since conquering Jerusalem, which worried many of the safety of Islam's third holiest site when they barely had enough time to lick their wounds and prepare for the defense. On July 22nd, in the streets of the city, Richard led the Christian army through the districts of Acre, which they had re-Christianized with crosses being raised above the reconsecrated churches. Eventually, they reached the main castle, where they established their headquarters.

Together with Philip II Augustus, Guy de Lusignan, Conrad of Montferrat, Henry of Champagne, Humphrey of Toron, Garnier de Nablus, Hugh of Burgundy, and the hundreds of nobles and high-ranking knights, Richard entered the castle. The English king then issued a joint statement to the coalition of the Third Crusade. Reminding them that it was only through God that their victory was made possible, the king declared that providence was on their side. And with it vested in their endeavor, the king pledged to remain in the Middle East, until Jerusalem had been reclaimed.

However, while these statements were received with broad support and enthusiasm by nearly every Crusader lord, the French king proceeded to unveil his own plans regarding his place in the Third Crusade. Philip II praised Richard's devotion, assuring him that he would pray for the triumph of his campaign. But, as for himself, Philip II stated that he believed that since Acre had been conquered, that his duties in the Holy Land were sufficiently met. He intended to return home to France. This, in the eyes of Frankish nobles, was an extremely unpopular move, tarnishing the image of Philip II for the rest of his life.

After four days, on July 26th, the council would convene again. Conrad of Montferrat had become politically isolated, and Richard forced him to return in submission. When they gathered once again, and Conrad was summoned before the coalition in the great hall of the castle, he protested. The departure of the King of France had left him without his largest sponsor, and so before everyone, he declared his claim to the throne of Jerusalem. The room erupted in ecstatic commotion. Nobles and knights voiced their support for Conrad, a far more preferable alternative to the throne of Jerusalem than Guy, who was still bearing the stain of Hattin's disgrace.

While Guy protested at this apparent threat to his status among the Crusaders, Richard would not back him unconditionally. The King of England sensed the popular sentiment in the room, and he would not be unwise to go against it just for his vassal. However, unlike the rest of the council, he was not entirely in favor of Conrad either. The king remembered that when his fleet first attempted to make landfall on the Holy Land, they arrived at the port of Tyre, but were denied permission by Conrad's men, forcing them to instead sail for Acre. Nonetheless, the king thought of what he needed to do to maintain the integrity of the Crusader coalition.

Thus Richard would present both men with his own proposal. Guy de Lusignan would have the throne of Jerusalem, but his successor would be Conrad of Montferrat. In the meantime, Conrad would rule Tyre, and Guy would also be awarded with the island of Cyprus. With both men satisfied with these terms, unity had returned to the Crusader camp for the time being.

Back in the Ayyubid camp, the Muslim leadership prepared for their departure. Acre was a difficult battle, but the war with the Crusaders was far from over. The men gathered their weapons and equipment, packing it and preparing to head on the march again, should the enemy press the offensive south. The sultan still anticipated the day of the long awaited prisoner exchange. Salahuddin dwelled on it heavily, but then made a calculation for how to manipulate the situation and bend it to his advantage. He told his scribes to delay their response to the Crusader camp. They would halt all communications. They were to stall them, prolong them, and insert new conditions. By delaying the exchange until autumn, they could buy time to gather more reinforcements and supplies.

From Acre's walls, Richard watched the field in the distance. It had been many days since his last correspondence with the sultan, and those days had passed dreadfully. He was growing impatient. Realizing that the sultan was intentionally obstructing the implementation of the agreement, Richard would take drastic measures. On the 20th of August, Richard herded some 2,000 prisoners onto the field outside the walls, before the army of Salahuddin. At that moment, upon Richard's orders, the Crusaders revealed their swords and began slaughtering the prisoners indiscriminately. The sultan was beyond infuriated. His cavalry, in an attempt to stop the massacre, charged with rage towards the field. The entire ordeal lasted throughout the afternoon, but the Muslim cavaliers were driven back by the Latin knights on horseback.

On that field, upon the completion of the massacre, all of the prisoners had been killed. Salahuddin, on the morning of the next day, resorted to equally gruesome ends. In response to Richard's act, Salahuddin had his own Frankish and Latin prisoners thrown in the sights of the Crusaders across the field. He had them all put to death. After the conclusion of this particularly brutal episode of violence, the sultan gathered his men and left Acre.

Part V
The Prevail
(1191 - 1193)

16th-century Turkish Cavalry Armor
The Louvre Abu Dhabi, UAE

Murad 211

Chapter 26
Blood Never Sleeps

Statue of Richard I, Palace of Westminster, London, UK

One of the quotes attributed to Salahuddin comes from when he supposedly spoke to his son about the consequences of war, telling him, "Son, I warn you against killing and shedding blood because blood never sleeps."

Salahuddin's entire career, from the day he left Syria to Egypt as a young officer in Nureddin's army, to his campaigns into the Muslim lands of the Levant, and finally his war with the Crusaders, had passed through years of war. The sultan understood that neither a state nor even a human being could survive for much longer if it continued down a path of perpetual conflict. War, as he correctly viewed it, begets more war.

Along the Mediterranean coast, the Crusader army began its advance. Nearly every Crusader lord had set out on the march under the leadership of Richard the Lionheart, all except Conrad of Montferrat, who returned to his power base in Tyre. The King of England led the army, galloping on his horse ahead of the coalition of Angevin, Frankish, Templar, Hospitaller, and Latin knights, along with additional Pisan, Sicilian, Norman, Anglo-Saxon, Briton, Flemish, Danish, and Genoese troops. Men, from nearly every nation in Europe, followed the English king down the coast. Even at the very shores of the beach, where the water of the sea met with the sand of the Holy Land, the men traveled in their disciplined formation with some marching along the water, the waves reaching at their feet.

Further out at sea, the Crusader fleet, carrying weapons and supplies, remained tethered to the shoreline and followed the army on their march. Likewise, the army also hugged the shoreline as well, seeking to remain as close to their supply ships as possible. However, the Crusaders had drastically slowed the pace of their march. Richard knew that the journey would be long and sought to ensure that his men had ample rest throughout the expedition. He also knew that his elite Latin knights would be fatigued in their heavy armor had he elected to march at great speed without stopping.

Meanwhile, Salahuddin was in the midst of his

defense preparations of southern Palestine. But it was unknown as to which target Richard would move against first, Askalan or Jerusalem. This was an intentional play of deception, as the Lionheart sought to either force the sultan to concentrate on one city or split his army to protect both. The sultan chose the latter option. In both Askalan and Al-Quds, Salahuddin organized his forces to bolster the garrisons' defenses of the two cities. Askalan and the holy city itself would be protected by 20,000 troops each. As for the city of Jaffa, the Sultan ordered for it to be destroyed. Neighborhoods were evacuated and relocated outside the city. The ramparts were brought down. Trees, gardens, wells, and anything of sustenance to the Crusaders were demolished. And the port itself had its infrastructure dismantled.

Salahuddin had elected to implement a scorched-earth policy, turning the land against the Crusader army, a major escalation in tactics. It was not the first time he had done it nor would it be the last. Meanwhile, further north, Richard continued his gradual march along the coast, eventually nearing the city of Haifa. His army's slow pace, which had gone on for weeks at this point, was in and of itself a painful measure inflicted on Salahuddin. Pressure was mounting on him to either engage or withdraw, as he could not sustain the impatience of his soldiers for much longer.

When the Crusader army was within reach of the city of Caesarea, *Qaysariah* in Arabic, some 20 miles further south from the Frankish position, the Muslim spies, watching from a nearby forest, ceased their activities and returned to their leader. In the mountains, Salahuddin was briefed on their findings. They anticipated that the Crusader army would divert away from the coast at one point in the road, where a hill would block their access to the beach. From there, they would travel on an open plain south of Caesarea.

Sensing an opportunity, Salahuddin sent out his cavalry to harass their columns on the open plain. In the afternoon, they descended down the mountain. The unsuspecting Crusaders were caught off guard, as the Muslims charged at them and fired volleys of arrows. As they scrambled to defend themselves, many were hit in the arrow barrage. Richard would act swiftly. On horseback, he led his Angevin cavalry to respond to the attack, meeting the Muslim riders in battle and routing them. The Crusaders had been weakened, and Richard could see it himself. After that short but threatening skirmish, he realized that he needed to divert the path of the army away from the threat of harassment. He then led them to the northern bank of the River of Reeds, a stream which flowed from inland and out into the sea. They rested on their side of it, buying their time and planning for their next move.

Across the river lies a plain called the *Rochetaillee*. Eyeing it for its suitable position, Richard planned to seize it. To reach the plain, however, he would need to cross the forest of Arsuf. This forest was one of Palestine's rare woodlands.

Shrouded in vegetation, the forest was feared by the Crusaders, who were wary of naively wandering through it when the threat of a surprise attack remained a present danger. Seeking to try his hand at diplomatic communications, Richard would dispatch a message to the sultan.

Several miles away, beyond the Arsuf woodlands, the Ayyubid camp had been established along a forested ridge to the east, overlooking the Rochetaillee plain. In the sultan's tent, Salahuddin and his small council gathered to discuss the letter sent by the English king. The king had requested diplomatic talks and permission to cross the Arsuf forest safely. The sultan, after listening to the news given to him, paused and planned, taking time to formulate his approach. He gave authorization to Al-Adil to meet with the king, but only so that he could stall and buy more time.

Uncertainty filled the minds of the leadership of the Muslim camp, as Al-Adil took to his horse and departed with his personal guards towards the Crusader camp. Salahuddin would return to his tent and continue the logistical preparations for the impending battle. That week, as negotiations were underway, he wrote to his brother, reminding him to prolong the negotiations and force the Crusaders to remain in their current position long enough for the Turkoman reinforcements to arrive from the north.

In the tent of the King of England, Al-Adil, known to

the Latins as *Saphadin*, was welcomed inside and was led to his seat before the king's table, which he stood at the other end of. As they both accustomed themselves to their seats and were offered water by the attendants, they each began preparing for the negotiations. Richard began by expressing his desire to come to a conclusive deal with the sultan to end the war.

Al-Adil responded, "King of England, if you wish to achieve peace, with myself acting as your intermediary with the sultan, then you must outline your conditions."
"The basis of the treaty must be this," Richard told him "You must return all the former lands of the Kingdom of Jerusalem to us and return to your own country."
Richard's demand could not have been any more audacious. Al-Adil himself would not tolerate the arrogance of it, and, on behalf of his brother, he had it rejected. Richard would not offer any other alternative. Thus Al-Adil promptly departed the camp, and the negotiations were over in an instant. That night, at the Muslim camp, when Al-Adil rejoined his brother, alarming news had arrived to the ears of the sultan. The Crusaders had crossed the forest.

When Salahuddin left his tent to catch a view of what had just transpired, from the hill at the edge of his camp, the sultan's eyes saw it. The Crusaders had pitched their tents and established themselves on the field before concluding for the night. Their fire-lit torches illuminated their presence in the land, as if fueling the rage of the sultan. The negotiations, initiated by Richard, had been a mere ruse, a distraction to cover his secret maneuver.

On September 7th, 1191, when dawn broke the next morning, the Crusaders initiated their walk. They formed up into their marching columns and trekked the land once more, now reorganized according to Richard's new instructions. Crossbowmen, archers, and speared infantry of all kinds shielded every side of the army not protected by the cover of the sea, essentially guarding the front lines and the flanks of the army. They were led by Henry of Champagne, stationed at the rear of the army, near the baggage and supply train for its protection.

At the right wing of the battle formation, four groups of Templar cavalry were mounted in their elite armor with some Briton and Angevin cavalry beside them. On the left wing, several groups of Hospitaller, Flemish, and Danish knights were led by Hospitaller Grandmaster Garnier de Nablus. At the core of the army was the king himself, Richard the Lionheart, surrounded by Angevin, Norman, Anglo-Norman, and elite Latin knights. Beside him was Guy de Lusignan.

As they passed through the fields of Arsuf, the Muslims were also preparing to launch their own offensive. Salahuddin and his army of warriors emerged and arrayed themselves into their battle positions with three distinct contingents. The central contingent was the elite Mamluk cavalry with some Syrian archers and infantry behind them.

Salahuddin himself commanded them alongside his Mamluk guard, accompanied by Al-Afdal. On their right flank was the assorted group of Egyptian cavalry and Nubian archers under Al-Adil. And on the other side, under the command of Gökbörü, alongside Taqieddin, the Turkic and Arab cavalry was assembled, accompanied by additional archers from the Jazira region and Iraq.

Numbering 25,000, the Muslim army far outnumbered the Crusaders, who had 15,000 at most. The sultan's army had been brought back from the brink with reinforcements from across the empire, and he had placed his prospects of victory on the advantage it gave him numerically. In the middle of the morning, when the sun's light had only begun to arrive from the horizon in the east, the sultan viewed his enemies once more and elected to initiate the battle. The Muslims began their assault. The infantry marched. The horsemen raced ahead. To intimidate their opponents, the Muslims chanted battle cries, banged their shields, and flew their banners to instill fear into the Franks and break their morale. The English king saw this and ordered his soldiers into their battle positions.

The Crusader troops turned to face the incoming hostility and firmly held their ground. The first outbreak of battle came when the Muslims started their attack with a barrage of arrows by the Mamluk cavalry. This bombardment of projectiles weakened the strength of the Crusader army, but they held on. The Egyptian right flank had quickly exerted significant pressure on the Crusader left wing. Egyptian cavalry had succeeded in encircling the left side of the Crusader army and were threatening the baggage train. In return, the Crusader crossbowmen fired back. Soon enough, however, as most of the troops took cover under their shields and armor from the arrow barrage of the Muslims, many grew impatient. The Hospitallers and their leader, Garnier de Nablus, were becoming uneasy and insisted that they break out of their formation and charge. It was then that he sent one of his knights to the king.

Richard demanded that they maintain their defensive position. The Hospitaller grandmaster refused and ordered his knights to disobey the king's orders. From the heart of the army, Richard witnessed the knights break his instructions. The grandmaster led the Hospitaller counter assault against growing Ayyubid harassment with many of the other groups joining them. Their energetic charge, filled with aggression and momentum towards their Muslim opponents, had driven back that respective wing of Salahuddin's army. But it also exposed a gap in Richard's coalition as well. When the king saw this, frustrated as ever, he realized that if he did not do the same, his army would be susceptible to a counter attack. The Hospitaller charge was against his orders, but he soon joined them with the rest of his men.

The king ordered his men to charge as well. He galloped on his horse and led his men out of their defensive positions and into the counterattack, driving the Muslim cavaliers away and killing a great many of them. The king himself plunged into the heat of the battle, engaging his enemy on horseback like a true warrior king. Salahuddin was appalled and saw the disaster that was feared to occur and ordered his commanders to regroup their forces.

Chaos had engulfed the entire battlefield, as the Crusaders' momentous charge increased in greater strength and intensity. The battle lines of the Muslims seemed to shatter with no hope of turning back the tide of the ordeal. Disorder and lack of communication crippled the sultan's army. Even his adviser, Bahaddin Ibn Shaddad, who had joined the sultan that day in battle, found himself separated from the core of the army. Bewildered and afraid, he retreated like many others, fleeing the violent scene. Many others were not as fortunate, as thousands of Ayyubid soldiers were slain and killed by the advancing Crusader knights.

On the far side, the one that dealt the momentous counterattack by the Templars, Gökbörü and Taqieddin found themselves on the ground, battling their enemies and slaying them where they stood. Beside them, many of the sultan's Kurdish and Turkic commanders were stationed together with them, and together they fought. Among them was Emir Musek Al-Mukhbir, one of the great Kurdish chiefs, Kaimaz Al-Adeli, one of the army's most respected Turkic commanders, and Lighush Al-Kurdi, another valiant military warrior of the Kurds. Under the leadership of Gökbörü, much of their men had been scattered across the forested area, but they persisted and continued to fight alongside the bravest of their men, the Turks and the Kurds of the Jazira region.

This battle alone saw the most violence of the entirety of the Third Crusade, entering a new phase, where the attacks became bloodier and the fighting more intense. Within the physical nature of medieval warfare, a soldier can use some bows and arrows to kill his enemy, keeping him at a safe distance. But in battles like Arsuf, where both armies find themselves confronting each other directly, no soldier is safe, and there is no such thing as distance or safety. A lot of the fighting is hand to hand with swords, knives, axes, spears, and even literal hands. The visceral nature of such violence has to do a lot with the physical force that is required to smash someone in the skull with an axe, slash their neck open with a sword, or stab them through the chest with a blade. These men, as they did centuries before and would for centuries to come, would look each other in the eyes and inflict horrific damage upon another human being, knowing well that, in the blink of an eye, they could suffer the same fate.

With the center army group under their command, Salahuddin and Al-Afdal rallied together the remnants of their once proud army and mounted a last, desperate attempt to halt the Crusader onslaught. The sultan led his final charge against the enemy. Despite unleashing a charge, fueled with bravery and tenacity, it failed to turn the battle's trajectory. Together with his troops, Richard the Lionheart met the

Muslim remnants head on and swiftly crushed their attempt. The sultan's force was routed. His Egyptian wing had been completely decimated. His Turkic wing from the Jazira had been driven away. And his center contingent had been devastated by Richard.

Long after the battle was over, Al-Afdal, with a bleeding wound on his forehead, rode into the vicinity of where the Jazira contingent made their last stand. The sultan followed close behind. They found Gökbörü and Taqieddin in the area, beside the bodies of their fallen martyrs. The sultan found the bodies of Emir Musek Al-Mukhbir, Kaimaz Al-Adeli, and Lighush Al-Kurdi, along with thousands more. Salahuddin was crushed. After months of constant setback, he lost yet another battle at Arsuf and yet more men, dearest to him. All three commanders had been exceptionally loyal to the sultan and celebrated within his army, with Emir Musek Al-Mukbir and Kaimaz Al-Adeli having supported the sultan in his rise to power for years.

The Battle of Arsuf witnessed the Muslims lose some 7,000 men, most of them having been from the Egyptian wing that was completely wiped out. On that day, September 7, 1191, Salahuddin had endured as great of defeat as he had encountered with the fall of Akka. Arsuf was by far the single bloodiest day for Salahuddin's army, far worse than even Montgisard. A great many men and horses had been lost.

These losses were recoverable, but the army was truly

in dire straits in the immediate aftermath of the battle. And the consequences of it stretched far beyond the Arsuf battlefield, penetrating deep into the very heart of Salahuddin's state, the leaders of whom nervously continued to place their hopes in the sultan's capabilities. If his image had not been weakened, then it was certainly shattered with the conclusion of the Battle of Arsuf.

Emerging from his misery, Salahuddin would move to recollect what remained of his army. Taqieddin, who fought alongside the men of the Jazira region, had been allowed to withdraw, and so he returned to Hama. The sultan's army would depart the area and cross a river, known as Al-Auja. In the hilly wilderness of Palestine, a place with lush, green grass on the banks of the river, a place of peace and refuge, the sultan made camp and had his commanders, along with every fallen soldier killed that day, buried in the soil. Resting on wooden stretchers and covered under white blankets, the sultan's commanders and several hundreds more were laid to rest in the Holy Land.

Those remaining with the sultan, his brother and son, stood by his side as they recited Al-Fatiha for their martyrs. As the men continued to rest, the sultan hiked to the top of a hill, which overlooked the river and the serene landscape that stretched into the vast distance behind it. When one of his commanders climbed the hill to inform him of the army's readiness to march once more, he found the sultan standing alone. In silence, he grieved the losses of so many of his men, as if they were his own children, his sons, his brothers. Returning to his place, as leader of the army, Salahuddin departed with his men, returning to the march south.

Taqieddin, in that same year, not long after he had retired from the war, became sick and died in Hama. News of this would reach Salahuddin on the road. It was yet another loss that had beset the grieving sultan. But it did not deter his resolve to defend Jerusalem with all he had left. His mission now concerned Al-Quds above all else, and so he rode south to bolster the defenses of Palestine for the war that he knew would arrive at its gates.

Chapter 27
The Struggle

Al-Qibli Mosque at Masjid Al-Aqsa, Jerusalem, Palestine

Across Palestine, the sultan and his men traveled fast. His devastating defeat at Arsuf was another damaging blow to the morale of his army, but his numerical losses were recoverable. His state, spanning the far-flung territories of Syria, Egypt, Yemen, northern Iraq, and the Hejaz, would support him with a nearly unlimited stream of fighters and supplies. After Arsuf, most of his army had been sent to Jerusalem, while he and a small division of lightly equipped soldiers sprinted further south into Palestine.

The Crusader leadership was beyond jubilant at the sight of the sultan hastily reorganizing his defenses. On September 29th, 1191, Richard and his army arrived outside

Jaffa. They found the city rising from the Mediterranean in smoke. Upon passing through its demolished walls, they found much of the city in ruins. Whole districts lay either trashed or in some locations, completely destroyed. The roads were littered with debris and much of the population had been moved elsewhere.

The demolition of Jaffa, however, was no detriment to the Crusaders from the long term outlook on the war. The king's army was well supplied with the Crusader navy still following them along the coast, ferrying them food and equipment at all times. Rebuilding Jaffa's fortifications was an affordable solution to Richard's army, and thus their efforts began to reconstruct what Salahuddin had left demolished. With no opposition from the Muslims in the fall of 1191, the Crusade finally turned inland, aiming at last for the holy city of Jerusalem.

Deep within the interior of Palestine, Salahuddin traveled with his bodyguard and a small portion of his army. He arrived at the city of Askalan, one of Palestine's last free ports, with a fateful decision. Realizing he could not defend both Al-Quds and Askalan, he would divert his resources and assets away from the latter option. Boldly demonstrating his willingness to abruptly change tactics once again, he ordered his army to completely demolish Askalan, just as he did with Jaffa. Again he brought down the ramparts, destroyed the wells, moved neighborhoods outside the city, and trashed the harbor.

The Arab spies continued to feed the sultan information from within the Crusader camp with one report speaking of Richard's plans to invade Egypt, Salahuddin's base of power. By destroying Jaffa and Askalan, the sultan had deprived Richard of inheriting the infrastructure to advance into Egypt. Off the coast of Askalan, Latin ships sailed near the port city, conducting reconnaissance to confirm the rumors that it was indeed demolished. Seeing the sultan's work for themselves, the sailors returned to Jaffa with the news. Having tried and failed to score a decisive victory against the Crusaders, Salahuddin would now commit himself to this scorched-earth policy for the rest of the war.

Later that month, the Crusader council convened in the king's tent. Richard's proposal to invade Egypt was met with resistance, as most of the nobles, such as Hugh of Burgundy, demanded that the king adhere to his Crusader duty to march on Jerusalem. With such intense and unyielding pressure from the council, the King of England was essentially forced to concede to their demands. The actual march on the holy city would not occur for several more weeks. The Crusader army, from Acre to Arsuf, had been exhausted and war-weary. To satisfy their desire for rest, Richard allowed them their due time to recover.

In this break, much to the disgust of some Christian onlookers, the Crusaders spent their time basking in the warmth of taverns and immersing themselves amongst the sin and filth of the newly erected pleasure houses of Jaffa and Acre. With the army polluted with alcohol and bogged down in this period of inaction and lethargy, Salahuddin saw an opportunity. He rode out from his camp towards the lands, situated between Palestine's deep interior and the coast. He traveled to the villages of Lydda, Ramla, Latrun, and Beit Nuba, demolishing the infrastructure, depleting the available food and water supplies, and destroying anything that could be of use to the Crusaders.

Finally, in October of 1191, the fighting season resumed. Richard, having replenished his forces, set out from Jaffa with his troops. The Muslims had left for the Crusaders an utterly desolate land, but the path inland towards the heart of Palestine was left open. And so the king's army began reconstructing a string of fortified sites, connecting Salahuddin's abandoned villages with the supply lines that ran from the coast. In this time that the Crusaders spent slowly rebuilding these sites, a number of small engagements broke out between the two sides. In addition to the scorched-earth policy, Salahuddin advanced his strategy with the adoption of hit-and-run tactics. Lightly-armored Muslim cavalry would attack and harass the Crusaders' construction efforts, inflicting occasional losses to hamper their progress.

Richard would join his men in responding to these threats, entering the heat of these incidents himself to drive away the Muslim attackers. Growing frustrated at the slow situation, Richard returned to his tent and entered diplomatic negotiations with the sultan, writing letters to him with the hopes of bringing the sultan to a deal before actually having to besiege Jerusalem. The sultan replied back with his own letters, but his aim was to stall for time, as he continued to bolster the defenses of Al-Quds.

For the next several days, both sides, as their leaders exchanged letters, would engage in episodes of sabotage and espionage under the cover of night. Salahuddin's Bedouin spies would sneak into the Crusader camp to rescue prisoners, while Richard would have pilgrims in disguise spy on the Saracen army and report back with critical information. Eventually, the sultan and the king came to agree that they should hold a round of negotiations. Thus the Muslim delegation under Al-Adil was sent to the Crusader camp once again at Yasur, where they would be welcomed to begin talks with Richard.

On this occasion, Al-Adil and Richard, unlike in previous engagements, began approaching one another on a more personal level. Both of them shared their interests and experiences in travel, cuisine, and hunting, topics which changed their perceptions of each other and allowed them to better respect one another as men. But then, Richard brought forth to Al-Adil his perspective on the war at hand, predicting that Salahuddin, just as at Acre, would not be able to defend and keep Jerusalem. Al-Adil, citing the near endless stream of resources and manpower from across the region, refuted this assertion. Becoming ever clear that both sides would not cease their commitment to owning Jerusalem, Richard would make a unique offer.

The king had proposed that Al-Adil take the hand of his sister, Joan. She had come with Richard on the voyage to the Holy Land, and ruled as Queen of Sicily. Al-Adil would of course be expected to renounce himself from Islam and convert to Christianity, but, through his marriage with Joan, he could rule an independent, neutral kingdom of Jerusalem. However, he had come with the intention to make progress on his brother's negotiations with the English king. The Crusader's proposed plan was far too drastic for him to accept, despite how generous it may have seemed. As a Muslim, who lived through the era of revival that produced the generation of Salahuddin, Al-Adil would neither give up his religion nor any of its holiest places.

After bidding each other farewell, Richard allowed Al-Adil to depart the camp with his men. Richard would watch, as his guest galloped away with his bodyguards, returning to his territory. For the next several months of 1191, Salahuddin and Richard would continue their letter correspondence, and, in order to extract a willingness to make concessions, Salahuddin began gesturing his diplomacy of generosity.

On one day, Richard experienced an accident on his horse when it injured itself, traveling over rough terrain, throwing Richard off of its back in the process. The sultan sent the king his physicians, two new, obedient horses, and some sorbet. After this chivalrous act, the two continued to write to each other, at which point the sultan described to Richard just how supported he was in his defense of Palestine, where he had the advantage of familiarity with the terrain, of being well supplied with food and men, and of being surrounded by his sons, family, and allies. The sultan then reminded Richard of just how far he was from his base of power, England and France, and how arduous of a task it would be for the Crusaders to regain Jerusalem. The King of England ultimately ignored the sultan's dissuasion and elected to progress with his advance in the Holy Land.

By November, the Crusaders had completed their defensive preparations at Yasur, moving on to seize the towns of Lydda and Ramla in the surrounding countryside. But with the onset of the ravaging winter that year, the Crusaders were beset with disease and faced appalling conditions. Many men and horses perished, but the resolve of the army to complete the Crusade, with the recapture of Jerusalem, still remained. After surviving six miserable weeks that winter, the Crusaders would gradually gain strength, taking Latrun and Beit Nuba before the final days of December.

In January of 1192, only twelve miles stood between them and the gates of Jerusalem itself. Every man in the Crusader army understood this, appreciating the great reality of just how far they had carried the Cross, some from across the entire known world, and how close they now stood to the cradle of their faith. For almost 100 years, European knights have lived through the same endeavor as their forefathers. Starting with the First Crusade of 1095, generation after generation of Crusaders would undertake the same arduous journey to Palestine. So many generations had ventured there that the Holy Land had become the graveyard for many of Europe's families. And this was a reality that many of those men and their families were conscious of. They would either conquer and settle in the land or die. And for the knights and soldiers, both outcomes would satisfy them.

On one snowy morning, Salahuddin's men stood above Jerusalem's fortified ramparts, looking out into the direction of the Crusader camp. Far off in the chilly distance, the leadership of that camp had made a decision, much to the outrage of the troops in the army. Richard, along with the Hospitallers, Latins, and Templars, had elected to go against the will of the Frankish nobles to lay siege to Jerusalem. For them, their rationale came from their logistical considerations. They could not lay siege to Jerusalem in the middle of winter, especially during conditions that would impede the delivery of supplies from the coast. Thus, they retreated back to Jaffa to recover and replenish what was lost that winter.

As the Crusader army returned back to the coastal lands, the damage done to the morale of the Third Crusade would be severe. Immediately following this event, the army scattered and fell into disorganization with many units heading for cities to the north, where food and drink were more plentiful. Meanwhile, on January 20th, Richard led his weakened force of Angevin, Norman, and Anglo-Saxon troops to seize the ruined city of Askalan, spending a great deal of time and resources repairing it.

In the north, division quickly became a major force in the internal affairs of the Crusade. Conrad of Montferrat had sent his Genoese sailors from Tyre to seize Acre for himself. Richard would learn of the news via a letter when his Pisan allies informed him of the attempt that Conrad's navy had made on the city, which was successfully thwarted when the Pisans fought them off and drove them away from the port.

Enraged by this unexpected incident, Richard and his army would furiously march north towards Tyre. However, Conrad too expected his arrival, and so he thus would set out with his Latin troops to meet him. Both factions would encounter each other on an open plain, halfway between Acre and Tyre. Richard and Conrad would ride ahead of their men to meet one another between the two facing armies that they had brought. From Conrad's position, he desired to further reassert himself as leader of the Crusaders, a status which he had believed was earned and thus why Acre deserved to be his. But Richard would not tolerate this dereliction of duty.

In a move to punish Conrad, Richard subsequently deprived him of his share of the revenues of the Crusaders' war profits. However, aside from severing him from the riches, Richard had no other means of truly disciplining Conrad, who still enjoyed the backing of his Latin allies from his power base in Tyre and his legitimacy to the throne of Jerusalem with his marriage to Isabella I, the second sister of Baldwin IV. This marriage practically made him an equal claimant to the throne as his rival, Guy de Lusignan. Conrad was now just as much Jerusalem's rightful heir as the former king.

However, Richard would not have much time to align himself with either side and allow such quarrels to consume his attention. The King of England would be delivered a message only to learn that, in Europe, his seat of power was in peril. His brother, John Lackland had aligned himself with King Philip II of France, seeking to usurp Richard's authority over the Angevin realm. Aquitaine, Normandy, and Anjou were all under threat from the conspiracy.

Richard understood the severity of the reality facing him. As the future of the Crusade was shifting more and more towards Conrad's hands and his power in the Angevin realm was slipping away, he judged that he needed to conclude his war in the Middle East immediately and return to Europe. He would embark on one last fighting season to capture Jerusalem and preserve the Crusade. In his tent, in Askalan, he would make a shocking reversal when he wrote to Conrad of Montferrat, promising him immediate rulership as King of Jerusalem.

In Acre, at the behest of Richard and the Crusader council, Conrad was crowned king. Six years after ascending to the throne of Jerusalem himself, Guy de Lusignan witnessed his crown wrestled out of his hands. He was more isolated than ever before. However, Conrad and Richard would come to a settlement with him. Richard assured Guy that he would be compensated. The King of England offered to grant him possession over Cyprus, thus he would become its king. With his interest piqued, Guy accepted the offer. This settlement finally restored stability to the Crusade and would lead to over a century of Frankish rule over Cyprus.

With Guy and Conrad's rivalry finally resolved, attention now turned back to Jerusalem.
Salahuddin had spent months in the holy city, refusing to ever leave it, fearing the possibility of its loss in any absence. In the day, he instructed his engineers to continue their efforts to bolster the city's fortifications and his soldiers to man them. And all throughout the night, he prayed with unending dedication inside Masjid Al-Aqsa, sleeping inside on a number of occasions. One night, he gathered with all of his commanders, whom he had summoned from across the empire, in his tent on the grounds of Al-Aqsa. Al-Adil, Al-Afdal, Gökbörü, Kotbeddin Zengi, Hossameddin Ibn Lajin, Mojahedin Berenkash, and all of the sultan's men were seated together in his tent, where not a single sound could be heard. With their very presence at such a significant place, they all understood the gravity of their duty to defend the Ummah.

As they continued to sit together in complete silence, the sultan finally broke it with his voice, when he said, "I will never leave Al-Aqsa. If it means my death, then I will die here."

Among his commanders were men, who were either family to the sultan, loyal allies of his, or once former opponents to his rule, who had bitterly fought against him, but would ultimately turn to become loyal supporters of his mission. That night, every one of them had pledged the same commitment to that cause. Further away, the Crusader political landscape had once again undergone dramatic shifts. Conrad of Montferrat had become King of Jerusalem. Salahuddin understood that, with a united coalition of Crusader nobles to support him, he would be the greatest threat to the Muslims after Richard's anticipated departure from the Holy Land. But that would quickly change.

In the evening of April 28th, Conrad walked through the quiet stone streets of Acre, eventually crossing paths with two strange, hooded men, dressed in black robes and cloaks. The Crusader king slackened his gate and greeted the pair, who he knew only as devoted Christian monks, supporting his cause to reclaim Jerusalem. But the two men suddenly revealed daggers and stabbed Conrad repeatedly in the chest. His Latin guards rushed to the scene and slayed one of the assailants, failing to catch the other, as he fled into the depths of the city's landscape. He was later hunted down and executed, revealed to be an agent of the Nizari Ismailis, the Order of Assassins, sent by Rashidadin Sinan from Masyaf Castle.

Rumors immediately spread, alleging the existence of a plot that was at play to murder the king-elect of the Third Crusade. Some of the Franks accused Richard, recalling his earlier power struggle with Conrad. Others, confidently believed it was Salahuddin, who sought to eliminate the threat that Conrad posed to him. And then there were some, who aimed their judgment towards Guy de Lusignan, whose rivalry with Conrad may not have entirely been settled. No matter what force behind the assassination was, Conrad of Montferrat was dead.

In Tyre, a council convened before the wife of the deceased king, Queen Isabella I. However, it took a drastic turn when several Latin nobles began arguing and bickering amongst themselves over who would succeed Conrad to the throne. Isabella I fought off these attempts and ultimately had her order imposed over the council.

She then received a message from Richard and delivered the news to the council, announcing that Henry of Champagne would marry her and thus succeed Conrad to the throne. Henry, who had been sent by Richard, quickly earned the allegiance of the majority of the Latin nobles and had secured his position as king-elect of Jerusalem, through his marriage to Isabella. The Lionheart, from his center of power in Askalan, had successfully navigated through yet another power struggle that threatened to derail the Crusade. He would, for the second and last time, direct his gaze back to conquest. Askalan's fortifications had been rebuilt, and he quickly prepared to advance on Gaza and the Ayyubid stronghold at Deir Al-Balah to the south. However, troubling news had arrived from Europe once again.

On May 29th, an envoy arrived at Askalon by sea with a message for the king himself. A council with the Crusader lords was convened. The envoy from Europe brought news of the treachery of Philip II of France. He, along with the king's brother, Prince John, put into action their alleged plot to overthrow Richard. His lands in Anjou, Normandy, and Aquitaine were now under threat. After strong advice from his council, Richard agreed to lead them one last time before he would return to Europe.

On June 6th, Salahuddin met with his spies on the walls of Al-Quds, informed by them
that the Crusader advance on the city was imminent. He was ready. His defenses had been upgraded and refortified continuously for months. However, while any assault on such a well guarded site seemed insurmountable, he also realized that the stable summer weather would aid the Crusaders to sustain a lengthy battle. Richard had long believed that attacking Egypt, the resource-rich heartland of Salahuddin's Muslim empire, was a far wiser course of action, but it would not only take years but also ignore the prime motivation for the Crusade, which was the zealous dream of reconquering Jerusalem.

With or without Richard, the Latins would march on the city for the Cross. And so Richard elected to properly lead them. The Crusaders began their summer offensive by advancing once again into the fortified towns of Latrun, Beit Nuba, and Beit Horon, passing through them in a matter of days. Soon however, Salahuddin's forces revealed themselves in the form of lightly-armored cavalry to delay the Crusaders on their journey. Richard would repel these attacks and throw himself into the midst of the fighting, succeeding in leading his men to a swift and short victory in destroying these cavalry parties. They also rapidly advanced to arrest and confiscate four Muslim supply caravans bound for Jerusalem. Its cargo, of which contained pack animals, weapons, food, and money, was now in Crusader hands.

Only nine miles stood between the Crusaders and Jerusalem. Some reconnaissance units had even reached the outskirts of the holy city itself, catching vivid glimpses of the Dome of the Rock, shining in the distance under the bright summer sun. With the imminent threat drawing near, the sultan took immediate action to prepare for the siege.

Chapter 28
The Warrior Sultan

15th-century Turkish Helmet, The Louvre Abu Dhabi, UAE

On that blistering summer day, the sultan, his commanders, and his army stood at the walled holy city and waited patiently for their enemy to arrive. Richard, upon arriving on the outskirts of the city, laid his eyes on Jerusalem and its seemingly impregnable fortifications. On July 4th, five eventful years after his victory at the Battle of Hattin, a miracle once again revealed itself upon the Muslims.

Salahuddin, watching from the walls, looked out to find the Crusader army in the far distance. They once again withdrew to the coast. Richard together with his men, looking at the city of Jerusalem for the first and last time, turned away. A siege, just by the apparent visual observations, would not yield victory for the Crusaders. If it did, it would take months, which Richard did not have. For him, he would leave the Holy Land, having restored Christian rule to vast portions of it, in Acre, Jaffa, and Askalan.

In the fortified defenses of Al-Quds, Salahuddin stood high on the walls with his brother and son, Al-Adil and Al-Afdal. Present among them was Gökbörü as well as Bahaddin Ibn Shaddad and Qadi Al-Fadil, whom the sultan had not seen in months. The sultan's commanders were gathering a 10,000 strong army, in preparation to return to the offensive, in light of the opportunity that emerged from Richard's departure.

The sultan and his commanders promptly armed themselves for the battle. They greeted their army of warriors with the image of strength, as they walked past them and mounted themselves onto their stallions. On the command of the sultan, the army set off across the land towards Jaffa. When they arrived in the afternoon, they seized a position on a hill located some distance outside of the city, granting them a commanding view over it.

It was July of 1192, and out of the scorching heat of the sun, the Crusader garrison on Jaffa's walls found themselves under attack with arrows flying at them from every direction. To alert the rest of the city, the defenders rang the alarm bells. At the scene of the attack, many were struck down during the barrage, but those who survived would not last for long either. Salahuddin had returned to waging war on the offensive. From beneath the walls, the defenders were caught off guard once again, as the Muslims scaled the city's fortifications and slaughtered their opponents. Along the walls, a fierce brawl would ensue, as the defenders fought hard and reinforcements were summoned to aid them in the defense. Then the gates were thrown open, as Salahuddin led thousands of his Mamluk horsemen to charge through the breach and pour into the defenses. Through the breaches, Salahuddin and his warriors stormed into the city and secured the walls.

The sultan and his troops had nearly defeated the enemy and driven them back to their castle, where they were trapped. And soon enough, the flags of Islam flew above the city's walls. As the defenders retreated to the castle and barricaded themselves in it, hundreds of remaining stragglers were abandoned outside and were stabbed to death by Salahuddin's army. Seeing his enemies hiding in the seaside fortress of the city, the sultan ordered his men to storm it. Under siege, the Crusaders of Jaffa managed to dispatch a message by bird to Acre. Upon discovering the news, Richard acted with haste.

At Acre, the Crusaders quickly assembled a fleet, composed of whatever ship was available to set sail across the Mediterranean coast, carrying less than even a third of the numbers that the Muslims had brought to Jaffa. In haste, Richard and his meager force sailed across the sea to Jaffa. Once they had arrived at the waters around the city, the

Crusaders caught sight of the Muslim banners, soaring over the walls. A sense of despair soon fell upon Richard's men, until one Christian soldier from the city swam across the water towards Richard's ship. Then suddenly, the whole crew on the Lionheart's galley noticed the swimmer next to their ship. They helped him climb aboard and sat him down on the deck to recover. When he was well tended to, Richard came to speak to him. He reported to the king that despite the city having been stormed by the Saracens, the castle had remained unconquered, as its defenders continued to resist.

In an act of the Lionheart's bravery, he brazenly leapt from his ship and plunged into the sea. In his armor, he swam through the tide to the beach. His men would all follow him. At the shores of Jaffa, for the last time, the Crusaders, drenched and exhausted from the swim, would form up their contingents and prepare for battle that late afternoon. Emerging from Jaffa's defenses, Salahuddin, Al-Afdal, and Gökbörü caught sight of them in the field. Riding out with the Mamluk cavalry, the sultan led his men to the hills in the east to reorganize his exhausted army. As Richard continued his march towards Jaffa, and the Muslims waited across the hills throughout the night, news came to Salahuddin from one of his spies in the morning. Crusader reinforcements were on the road from Caesarea, aiming to join Richard's army. He would not allow it.

In the morning of August 4th, he lifted his sword to

the skies and gave the order to his army. In one momentous charge, the sultan and his men would unleash upon their enemies one last cavalry assault to secure the fate of the Holy Land. In the field outside Jaffa, both sides met in battle and fought ferociously. Both sides suffered casualties and were utterly exhausted, as Mamluks failed to break through the armor of the knights, while the Crusaders could not muster assaults of their own to decisively deal a great enough blow to the Muslim cavalry.

It came to an end when the Muslims withdrew from the field, after being routed by the tenacity of Richard's soldiers. They had fought each other to a stalemate with neither side gaining victory over the other. When it was all over and a quiet wind descended over the field, neither side had won. Many Muslims and Christians perished together, sharing the ground where they died. By the late afternoon, Jaffa's fields were littered with the dead and dying.

Chapter 29
The Return

Jaffa, Palestine

The Battle of Jaffa would be the last military engagement of the Third Crusade, as both monarchs, Salahuddin and Richard, moved to secure a diplomatic settlement to end the war in the Levant. In Salahuddin's camp, the sultan, together alongside his closest advisers, Al-Adil, Imadeddin Al-Isfahani, Qadi Al-Fadil, and Bahaddin Ibn Shaddad, received the Frankish delegation sent by Richard in his tent. Balian of Ibelin led the king's efforts to strike a deal, marking this occasion as the second time Balian had come to the sultan, asking for terms of peace.

Richard, still carrying inside him a desire to properly experience Jerusalem, wrote to the sultan, telling him, "I see that I shall never take Jerusalem, since you are resolved not to surrender it. But I am also resolved never to leave the land without having been inside the holy city. If then I cannot enter it as a conqueror, permit me to enter it as a pilgrim."

Salahuddin, as recorded by Imadeddin Al-Isfahani, replied back, "The city is ours in the same way that it is yours. We cannot grant *you* entry, for if we did, you would not be content unless you took possession of it. But I will grant entry to your people, for I know that in your heart you desire only pilgrimage."

The condition that Christians be given safe passage as pilgrims, traveling to the Church of the Holy Sepulcher free of restriction, was a matter of immense importance to the Crusaders. The king along with the rest of the Crusader council also sought to retain all of their holdings in Palestine. Tyre, Acre, Haifa, Caesarea, Arsuf, Jaffa, and Askalan were to be recognized as Crusader possessions. In the Crusader camp, a sickly and battle-wounded Richard sat exhausted in his tent with his Latin nobles, where he received Salahuddin's ambassador, Al-Adil.

The Sultan of Egypt and Syria demanded three years of peace. Askalan's fortifications were to be vacated and demolished. They would allow Christian pilgrims to visit Jerusalem, just as they always have, and the Franks would retain control of the coastal cities. As for Jerusalem, it would be left to remain under the rule of the Muslims. In both tents, identical copies of the treaty were presented before both factions. Salahuddin agreed with Balian, and Richard agreed with Al-Adil. Then, with both delegations bearing witness, each side swore their oaths. Commanders and key figures from both armies, such as Balian of Ibelin, Al-Adil, Henry of Champagne, Muzafferidin Gökbörü, Richard, and of course the sultan himself all swore to the pledge of peace.

The letters were signed on September 2nd, 1192. With the conclusion of the treaty, the war had ended along with the Third Crusade. Palestine, for the first but not the last time in its history, had effectively been partitioned with the Crusaders gaining the narrow coastal strip from Tyre to Askalan, while the Muslims retained control over the heartland, including Jerusalem. Having agreed to this compromise, Salahuddin had successfully protected and secured Islamic rule over Al-Quds, which would continue for over seven centuries. At the city of Acre, Richard passed through the harbor with his knights and arrived at his ship.

But before he left the Holy Land, Salahuddin, perhaps both from a place of kindness and a necessity to maintain good relations, would conclude his relationship with Richard when he wrote to him, "If I were to give up the Holy Land, I would give it to no one but you."

The sultan's diplomacy seemed to have left a significant impression on Richard. The King of England, in all his travels from Europe to the Holy Land, would not find any man equal in character to the sultan.

Around the time that he and his men sailed to Europe, Richard reportedly remarked, "Saladin is the finest king I have ever met."

    He would never have his face-to-face meeting with Salahuddin, despite his many attempts to do so. And while the sultan and his nation belonged to religion and civilization, that was and would, for centuries to come, be disparaged and vilified by the West, the Christian king himself recognized that he had never encountered a more honorable adversary. And so Salahuddin, through his interactions with Richard, may have been the first Muslim to at least soften Europe's perception of the Muslim world, demonstrating a rare kind of chivalry, mercy, and respect in a way that challenged the prevailing image of the Muslims as a barbarous people. The King of England would continue on his long journey across the Mediterranean. Salahuddin simultaneously began his own journey, riding back to Syria.

    The war was over, and the sultan's mission of guarding Al-Quds had been fulfilled. He and his entourage intended to return to Damascus to receive a great welcome for their victory. Though, while they traveled on the road, at a slow pace, Salahuddin began wheezing and eventually coughing. His illness had not been cured by his physicians. It continued throughout the course of his war with the

Crusaders. Finally, when they had reached the outskirts of Damascus, the sultan was welcomed back to his capital.

However, not long upon his arrival, news had spread that the sultan had fallen seriously ill. For two weeks, he suffered from intense fever. Confined to his sleeping quarters and sweating under his sheets, his physicians treated him and reported of the unbearable headaches and indigestion he felt, to the point where stopped eating. In an almost parallel manner to Khalid Ibn Al-Walid, the warrior sultan would not die in a battlefield, but instead in his bed.

In documenting some of his last words, Bahaddin recorded the sultan to have remarked, "Let there be carried before my bier a piece of the shroud in which I am to be buried, so that men may see that the King of the East could take nothing with him to the grave."

Near to his death, the sultan would forgo all attachment to his wealth and surrendered himself to the humility of the Sunnah. His character had been shaped as such from the beginning of his career until its very end. As the hafez recited Quran beside his bed, Salahuddin would slowly drift in and out of consciousness, occasionally twitching, mumbling, and reacting to certain verses of the Quran, which he himself had memorized devotedly.

Then a silence descended upon him, and the sultan, at the age of 56, drew his last breath. On March 4th, 1193, Salahuddin Yusuf Al-Ayyubi, the Sultan of Egypt and Syria, died. He was buried outside Masjid Al-Umawi, the Umayyad

Mosque. The people of the city and those beyond it, in Cairo, Jerusalem, Aleppo, Mosul, Medina, and Mecca, mourned and publicly grieved his passing. No wealth was left in his coffers. He had spent his entire fortune, from the revenues of his vast domain, generously donating charity to the poor. The last of his property amounted to one gold dinar and 40 silver dirhams, along with his horse, armor, and swords. Qadi Al-Fadil had granted unique permission for the sultan to be buried with his sword, an exception within what Islamic law permits in the burials of Muslims.

And when his body had finally been laid down in the ground, a solemn realization had come upon the people. They would never live to see a leader like him for a long time. In the centuries that would pass, his legacy, embodied in his unification of the Ummah and the liberation of Al-Aqsa, would be greatly revered by the Muslims, regarding him amongst the greatest leaders of Islam, Abu Bakr, Omar, Uthman, and Ali (رضي الله عنهم), the first rightly-guided caliphs after Prophet Muhammad ﷺ. And when he passed, the people made dua that God, just as He had opened for him the doors of Jerusalem, would open for him the doors of Heaven.

In their imagination, his feats made him the greatest leader they had seen since the Prophet ﷺ and the first four caliphs that succeeded him. However, none of those feats would have been possible without the generation that fostered the movement of revival in the Muslim world. From the humble carpenters, who built the minbar for Al-Aqsa, to the scholars who educated entire generations in the curriculum of Sunni revivalism, to Imadeddin and Nureddin Al-Zengi's establishment and consolidation of the Zengid state, to the many army commanders, soldiers, and statesmen of the Ayyubid Sultanate, it was the generation of Salahuddin and the generations before them that made the liberation of Jerusalem possible, preserving it as the right of the Ummah for centuries to come.

Chapter 30
The Revival

Hagia Sophia Grand Mosque, Istanbul, Turkey

"Verily, you shall conquer Constantinople. What a wonderful leader will that leader be, and what a wonderful army will that army be."

لَتُفْتَحَنَّ الْقُسْطَنْطِينِيَّةُ، فَلَنِعْمَ الْأَمِيرُ أَمِيرُهَا، وَلَنِعْمَ الْجَيْشُ ذَلِكَ الْجَيْشُ

- Prophet Muhammad ﷺ [Musnad Ahmad Ibn Hanbal 18189]

In 1193, the Treaty of Jaffa had been ratified. Jerusalem was securely under Muslim rule. And Salahuddin had gone.

With the sultan's death, it soon became apparent that no one could assert themselves within the void left by his passing. In regards to his state, spanning much of the region, it would neither possess any resemblance to his leadership nor withstand the test of time for long.

His empire would be divided amongst his quarreling family members, who ruled over it for the next six decades. The governorships of Egypt, Damascus, Aleppo, and other provinces of the state would be contested back and forth between the sultan's sons, Al-Afdal, Al-Aziz, Az-Zaher, and their uncle, Al-Adil. Out of the internal power struggles, Al-Adil emerged as the most capable ruler with his position as Sultan of Egypt elevating his authority over the rest of the Ayyubid realm. But even with his rule over the quarreling brothers, his ability to govern would not solve the division that had been inflicted upon the state. And the Crusaders, having been allowed to retain possession of Jaffa, Acre, and much of the coast in the treaty of 1192, remained a present threat to the Muslims.

Barely 40 years after Salahuddin's death, one of his nephews, Al-Kamil, the son of Al-Adil, was pressured into negotiating a treaty with the army of the Sixth Crusade, resulting in the voluntary surrender of Jerusalem back to the Crusaders. Such a betrayal of Salahuddin's legacy would not last for long, and the Muslims soon regained the city after this short-lived humiliation with the recapture of Jerusalem in 1244.

In 1250, the decaying Ayyubid state, which had largely become less capable of governing the region, was deposed. A group of Mamluk generals, the elite warrior class that supported and fought for Salahuddin, seized power in Egypt and brought the Ayyubid state to its end. In its place, they established the Mamluk sultanate, known officially as *Dawlat Al-Atrak*, "the State of the Turks." However, by this point, despite the return of stability under the strong leadership of Mamluk military rule, the internal fragmentation of Salahuddin's former domain would cripple the region just before the onset of another calamity.

In the face of the tidal wave that was the brutal Mongol invasion, which saw the destruction of Baghdad and the Abbasid Caliphate in the most gruesome and appalling episodes of human crime, it would be yet again the Mamluk warrior class, who spearheaded the resistance. The Mongols had allegedly slaughtered between 800,000 and 2 million of the city's inhabitants with the caliph among them. Perhaps even worse than Jerusalem in 1099, the Mongol desecration of Baghdad not only claimed the lives of hundreds of thousands of people dead but also left the city in complete ruin. Knowledge and research, stored in the books of Baghdad's House of Wisdom, were also destroyed, a true loss for the advancement of human civilization. It is even said that the Tigris River ran black with the ink of those books. The Mongols then proceeded to conquer the rest of Iraq and move into Syria, entering Damascus and Aleppo, where they also repeated some of the same atrocities.

Seeing the region fall to these hordes, the Mamluks set out with an army from Egypt to meet the Mongols in battle. In the Battle of Ain Jalut, where David is said to have vanquished Goliath, the Mamluks of Sultan Qutuz and Baibars defeated the Mongol army in the fields of Palestine. With their defeat, Syria would be returned back to Muslim rule. Under the rule of Sultan Baibars, who seized power from his master, Qutuz, he would lead the Mamluks to resist the Mongols, reducing the threat they posed to the region with each and every defeat inflicted upon the newly created Mongol Ilkhanate of Iran. Before the end of the century, with the Mongols having been kept at bay, the Mamluks finally defeated the last of the Crusaders with the capture of Acre in 1291. Because of the Mamluks, the Crusades were brought to an end, and the land of Greater Syria would exist under the stable rule of their state, which anchored its base of power in Egypt.

However, the reclamation of Al-Aqsa and the reunification of the heartland of the Muslims would not be the end of Islam's revival. Salahuddin had dreamt, like many leaders of his time, that once Jerusalem had been reclaimed, the Muslims would continue to consolidate strength amongst themselves, under a powerful leadership that would lead them to expand Islam across the globe. And because of the feats of his reign and his generation, that revival would not stop.

In the 15th century, a new Muslim superpower was on the rise. From a small beylik, consisting of two villages in Anatolia, to one of the world's most long-lasting empires, spanning three continents and even larger than the Romans, the Ottoman Empire was poised to assume the mantle of leadership over the Islamic world. Strength was rooted within the very spirit of the Ottoman State. Osman Gazi, the founder of this state, started from a tiny village. The Ottomans had nothing to begin with and began their history caught between empires and entities far stronger than they were. Just like Salahuddin, who began his life as a refugee, fleeing Iraq, many of the early Ottomans were nomads, who fled to the western edges of Anatolia to escape the Mongol onslaught. Yet, through their subjugation of the various Turkic beyliks in Anatolia and their conquest of Byzantine territory in Europe, they set themselves on a course that would see them come to dominate the world and make themselves into a superpower.

For Europe, it would prove to be a superpower, so catastrophic that even Pope Pius II would remark, "A disaster has fallen upon all of Christendom with the loss of Constantinople."

In 1453, the 800-year-old prophecy by Prophet Muhammad ﷺ, that the Muslims would one day conquer Constantinople, finally came true with the victory of Sultan

Mehmed II, who would end the Romans at the walls of the city. On May 28th, the last stand between the Romans and their 800-year-old adversary, the Muslims, was at hand. Ever since their first battle at Mu'tah, the Muslims had come a long way before they would finally complete their conquest of the greatest empire of the ancient world.

Cannon fire filled the air, as the Turks relentlessly launched wave after wave of assaults, until they breached the defenses and flooded into the walls of Constantinople in the thousands. The last emperor, Constantine XI, saw that as his city fell, so would he. He would meet the Turks in battle, and, in the chaos of the siege, he would never be seen or heard of again. With his death, the Roman Empire, the once great empire of the Mediterranean, finally met its end.

On May 29th, Sultan Mehmed II rode on horseback into Constantinople. On that day, he was only 21 years old. And in light of his triumph, he declared himself *Kaiser-i Rum*, meaning "the Caesar of Rome." Following this day, he would be known to history also by another name: *Fatih*, "the Conqueror." Constantinople, the second Rome, would be transformed into the capital of the new Muslim state, the city of Istanbul. The city of the Romans, whose population and infrastructure had declined since the Fourth Crusade, when the city was sacked and plundered by the Latins, would be repopulated and renovated by the Ottomans. The prize of the city itself, the Basilica of Hagia Sophia, would be transformed into a grand mosque. But the Ottomans would not stop at Istanbul.

In 1517, the grandson of Mehmed II, Selim I, conquered Egypt and Syria, bringing them along with Mecca and Medina under the Ottoman Empire. With that achievement, Selim, his son Suleiman, and their successors would enthrone themselves at the head of their new Ottoman Caliphate. Mehmed, Selim, and Suleiman all lived within a century and reforged the Ottomans from a regional power into *the* superpower of the world, completing the true revival of the Ummah that began with the generation of Salahuddin.

This empire was the dream of every Muslim ruler, breathed into life. It ruled the Balkans, Anatolia, the Caucuses, Syria, Iraq, Arabia, Yemen, Egypt, Libya, Tunisia, Algeria, and far beyond. It administered over Muslims, Christians, Jews, Turks, Greeks, Armenians, Bulgarians, Hungarians, Romanians, Serbs, Bosnians, Albanians, Arabs, Berbers, Kurds, Circassians, Chechens, Tatars, and numerous other peoples within the empire's borders. The Black Sea, the Red Sea, the Gulf, the Aegean, and the east of the Mediterranean were dominated by the Turkish crescent flag for centuries. Even as far as Aceh, in Indonesia, did the empire expand its reach. From the outskirts of Vienna to the island of Sumatra, from the Atlas Mountains of Algeria to the Gulf of Aden, from the woods of Crimea to the bustling streets of Cairo, and from Hagia Sophia in Istanbul to the

Kaaba in Mecca, this Ottoman Empire carried its flag in all directions.

The Ottoman ascendency onto the three continents marked a second era of Muslim dominance on the world stage, a second golden age. While it would contend with Safavid Iran for well over a century, and while it certainly would not unite the entirety of the Muslim world, the Ottoman Empire was nonetheless the most realistic perfection of Islamic rule. On the empirical level, it combined military strength, vast territorial expansion, and economic prosperity through the control of major arteries of trade like the Mediterranean, the Red Sea, the Indian Ocean, and the Silk Road, making it the leader of global commerce, only perhaps rivaled by Spain and Portugal's economic monopoly over the Americas.

As for what its rule represented, leaders like Mehmed II, Selim, Suleiman, and Murad IV upheld Islamic law, while fostering a multiethnic and multireligious society, in line with the Islamic tradition. They built magnificent mosques and madrasas, rewarded the scholars, legislated legal reforms, and united various cities, lands, and peoples under the stability of its state. To compliment its prestige and dominance on the globe, the Ottoman State was equally so, in the exemplification of the morals and principles of the Quran and the Sunnah within its leaders and institutions, a truly Islamic state. It perfected itself in becoming *Devlet-i Aliyye*, "the Exalted State."

According to Turkish academic, Professor Ekrem Bugra Ekinci, "Preserving and propagating the Aqa'id (beliefs) of Ahl Al-Sunnah wa'l Jama'ah was the sole aim of the Ottoman State from its start to the end."

There is no doubt that this model of a state was what Salahuddin envisioned when he spoke of reviving the Ummah and spreading Islam throughout the world. And in fact, this Ottoman future would never have been possible without the achievements of Salahuddin, his generation, and the generation of Muslims before him. The seeds of revival were planted all those years ago when the Seljuks and Zengids built madrasas, in 11th-century Baghdad and Damascus, to guide the Muslim youth to reteach the creed of Islam in its purest form. By educating the Muslims and forcing them to rediscover what they were truly about, could leaders like Nureddin Al-Zengi initiate that revival, could Salahuddin Al-Ayyubi achieve that revival, and could Mehmed, Selim, and Suleiman spread that revival across the world.

And so for over 400 years, as this caliphate of revival spread and defended Islam across the continents and the oceans, the heartland of the Ummah, the land of Greater Syria, that Salahuddin had unified and freed from the Crusaders, would continue to remain under the ownership of the Muslims, who would inherit the legacy of revival for centuries to come.

Epilogue
The Modern Middle East

Mausoleum of Salahuddin, Damascus, Syria

The Ottoman manifestation of the Muslim revival would, after its ascendancy onto the world stage in 1517, last for 400 years. These four centuries would of course come to an end. It would decline for several decades, until it was firmly brought to an end with the events of 1917. Over 700 years after Salahuddin, the old world of the sword and horse had gone, replaced by the mechanized industries of a new Europe. Secular liberalism had replaced religion in the courts of power. And the caliphate, resting in the hands of the last absolutist Ottoman sultan, Abdulhamid II, was stripped of its power and regulated to a ceremonial authority. This act was carried out in the 1908 coup by the Young Turks, Muslims, who pursued the vision of a nationalist Turkish state, one which alienated the Arabs, but also the Armenian and Greek minorities that had lived and coexisted with the Muslims for centuries.

In 1914, the First World War had erupted, and its fire quickly reached the Middle East to burn down the declining Ottoman Empire, which entered the conflict on the side of the Central Powers. The British and French, long remembering their crusading history in the Levant, returned with renewed imperial ambitions. After defending the homeland at the beaches of Çannakale from the Allied Gallipoli Campaign, which ended in 1916, and repelling British military operations upon the borders of the state, in Iraq and Palestine, the defeat of the Ottomans would come when an Arab revolt, aided by Britain, finally overwhelmed it.

On December 11th, 1917, the British army commander, General Edmund Allenby, entered the holy city of Jerusalem. On foot with his expeditionary force, he walked through the city, claiming it for Britain. From that day forth, the Ottoman Empire would continue its fall to defeat, and Palestine would exist under British occupation.

On the day he entered Jerusalem, Allenby reportedly remarked, "The wars of the Crusades are now complete." What followed would mirror the events of 1099 with the First Crusade, only this time, the Europeans executed their colonial vision of the Middle East through far more calculated, methodical, measured, and disciplined means. While the Arabs of the revolt against the Ottomans were promised a state, the West would only reward them with betrayal. While Faisal I, the son of the Hashemite ruler of Mecca, Sharif Hussein bin Ali, would be made King of Syria and ruled the country alongside the Arab National Congress, this only lasted for just the summer of 1920.

While the British occupied Palestine and the French Lebanon, Faisal's newly created government in Damascus failed to administer the wartorn and economically devastated country. With France's further encroachment upon Syria, the Arab National Congress, against the will of Faisal, elected to respond and declared war. After these attempts were thwarted by the French in the Battle of Maysalun, France's 415th Infantry Battalion of the Levant drove its convoy of vehicles into the capital of the Arabs, Damascus.

Faisal was forced to flee. His government disintegrated. And on that day, General Henri Gouraud, arriving in a car, paid a visit to the tomb of Salahuddin outside Masjid Al-Umawi. In that infamous moment, the French general was alleged to have arrogantly kicked the grave of the Muslim leader and invoked the same Crusader mentality of civilizational war, of a clash of civilizations.

He is rumored to have said, "Awake, Saladin. We have returned. Our presence here marks the victory of the Cross over the Crescent."

The French general then left the tomb, returning with his men to their convoy and driving away to tour the rest of the city. In the occupations that followed, the French and British would erect mandate systems to govern Palestine, Jordan, Syria, Lebanon, and Iraq. The Balfour Declaration of 1917, the British promise of facilitating the establishment of a Jewish national home in Palestine, materialized in 1948. That year witnessed the creation of the State of Israel, a state which was simultaneously created alongside the expulsion of 750,000 Palestinian Arabs from their homes in what is known in the Arab world as the *Nakba*, the "Catastrophe." Israel, in its early years, even while being surrounded by Arab adversaries on all sides, who at least in name supported the Palestinians, still managed to extinguish these threats and expand its borders, eventually seizing control over the entirety of the country after the war of 1967, from the Jordan River to the Mediterranean coast. Its occupation over the Palestinians has led to decades of tension in the region, which still remain unresolved. Once again, Jerusalem and Al-Aqsa, had been lost.

No lasting, unified Arab nation would emerge, despite vigorous efforts by Arab nationalists to create one in the 20th century. And the caliphate, a position wielded by the Ottoman sultans for 400 years and a title held by the Muslims for over a thousand, was abolished in 1924 by the newly founded Republic of Turkey, terminated by Muslims themselves, who pursued the West's invention of secular nationalism as the ideal model of governance.

But in the new nation states throughout the Muslim world, these new political traditions of modernity, secularism, and nationalism would not protect them. They would not guard their societies from the tyranny of despotic leaders, nor from the danger of terrorist groups, and not the least from the military interventions of Western governments, whether with the British, French, and Israelis in Egypt during the 1956 Suez Crisis or with the US-led invasion of Iraq in 2003.

According to the late Turkish writer, Ustadh Kadir Mısıroğlu, "Those who destroyed the Ottoman State have taken the fur of the lion and given it to forty foxes (i.e nation states). But not even one of them could succeed in becoming a baby lion."

Following the demise of the Ottoman Empire, the division of the Arab world, and the loss of Jerusalem to the State of Israel, many experts, both within and beyond the Middle East, have attempted to diagnose the central issue that has caused the region to undergo such dramatic turbulence after World War I. But from all the conclusions that can be made, one fact remains certain: secularism and nationalism in the Arab world has been a disaster, and it wasted the 20th century.

For decades, after states gained their independence from European rule after World War II, Arab nationalism emerged as a movement that promised prosperity, strength, and modernization under a united Arab state. And it failed. It would instead produce division, authoritarianism, and stagnation. Unlike states such as Turkey, which successfully implemented its own nationalism to strengthen its nation, Arab nationalism failed to deliver solutions to an already fractured region and ultimately hindered its development. From its inception in the midst of World War I to its decline after 1967, Arab nationalism would rest at the center of Middle Eastern geopolitics for over half a century and then crumble in the face of internal divisions and poor leadership, leaving the Arab world in a state of perpetual crisis.

    The roots of Arab nationalism can be traced to the midst of the First World War, when the British government instigated the Arab revolt against the Ottoman Empire. Instead of granting the Arabs and the Hashemite royal family an independent state as promised, the UK along with France went ahead to impose their mandates over the newly drawn Middle Eastern territories. This move effectively divided the region into artificial nation-states, essentially the skeleton for the borders of the region, causing many issues in the long term. This was unlike Turkey's experience with nationalism. Despite its eventual de-Islamization of old Ottoman society, Turkey was united under the leadership Mustafa Kemal Atatürk in 1923, who through his military offensives against Greece and France, was able to reject the division of Anatolia and establish a secular republic.

In contrast, when secular nationalism entered the imagination of the Arab world, it was introduced to a region that was already broken into numerous fragmented polities. Because the Arab world had been divided between multiple states, especially in the Middle East, the Arab nationalist movement remained more of a popular idea rather than a functional political reality. The failure of Arab nationalism to unite the Arab people was most evident in the creation and collapse of the United Arab Republic.

Championed by President Gamal Abdel Nasser, the UAR was created with the unification of Egypt and Syria under a single state, the *Wahdeh* or "Union" of 1958. It was a historic move, but upon Syria's incorporation into the United Arab Republic, it faced immediate challenges. Syria's economy was far more modern than impoverished Egypt. A middle and an upper class of entrepreneurs and businessmen thrived there. Now part of this Arab union, Syria's wealth was being used by the socialist Nasser administration to solve the poverty crisis in Egypt, at the expense of Syria's economy. Under President Nasser, Syrians were feeling the pressure of overwhelming Egyptian influence over their country. Thus in 1961, within just 3 years, Syria withdrew from the union.

This failure highlighted the fundamental problem of Arab nationalism. Rather than unifying the region, because of poor leadership and often socialist-leaning policies, it exacerbated existing tensions between Arab states. It even worsened relations, as was the case with monarchies like

Saudi Arabia and Jordan. In fact, in response to the UAR, Jordan and Iraq, both ruled by Hashemite monarchies, attempted to forge their own union, but this too was unsuccessful due to disputes over leadership. Who would lead and whose vision would prevail proved to be the points of contention that ultimately derailed any attempt to unite.

Unlike Turkey and even Iran until 1979, which were led by strong, effective leaders, and who used nationalism to great effect within their borders, Arab nationalism aimed for an unrealistic pan-Arab unity. Maps from this period illustrate an Arab state that stretches from Oman to places as far away as Mauritania. Such a vision, one which was secular in nature, would never be achieved and could only be used as propaganda pieces.

Arab nationalism was also used, and at times abused, to give rise to authoritarian regimes. As seen with Nasser, but also in the cases of Saddam Hussein and Hafez Al-Assad, they used nationalist rhetoric to validate their rule with the latter two suppressing dissent and consolidating power in appallingly brutal fashion. In fact, all three leaders would employ similar methods of propaganda, giving legitimacy to their rule by likening their image to that of past Arab leaders like none other than Salahuddin Al-Ayyubi. This was where the legacy of the sultan of revival was reinvented, as seen with the coat of arms for many of these Arab leaders, which depicted the eagle, the symbol of Salahuddin's dynasty. And in Damascus, Baghdad, Cairo, and elsewhere, artists began depicting the sultan in movies, illustrations, and even statues. No longer was he the Muslim leader, who exemplified the teachings of the Quran and the Sunnah to unite the region and liberate Al-Aqsa. Rather, he was reinterpreted as a nationalist hero, an 800-year-old character of past glory.

But as with the hollow nature of this kind of secular nationalism, none of these ideas or interpretations truly mattered. They were all symbolic in nature, meant to give credibility around the cult of personality of a dictator. And this was no more evident than in the barbarism of the regime of Hafez Al-Assad and his son Bashar. Their 53-year rule of tyranny over Syria forced upon Syrian society an era of silence, oppression, mistrust, and isolation from the rest of the world. From Hama in 1982 to Daraa in 2011, the regime's war against its own people, who only asked for justice, freedom, and a better life, devastated the nation and destabilized the entire region. Since 2011, when the civil war began, millions of Syrians have been either killed or forced to flee as refugees, turning the idea of Syria, in the eyes of the world, into one of tragedy and horror. 2011 was the year the Middle East imploded. And the events of that year and the decade that followed would also greatly affect the internal stability of Europe. A direct line can be drawn from the conflicts of the Middle East to the refugee crisis that destabilized Europe.

However, it remains to be asked: how did Syria, in

particular, reach this point? How did this country, which, out of all the Arab nation-states, could have been one of the most successful countries in the region, fall so far? It began when secularism and nationalism were sown into the political and social identity of the state. Syria, since its independence from French mandate rule in 1946, had been a secular country. Islam was divorced from the legal fabric of the government. And thus, with the rise of a nationalist political party, such as the Ba'ath Party of the Assad regime, Syria would be administered by a government that had no sense of Islam's justice.

The principles from the Quran and the Sunnah, which were instilled in generations of Muslim leaders from the Sahaba to sultans, were completely discarded by a regime that had no moral center, not even a true ideological mission. The only purpose of the regime in Syria was to keep the Assad family in power and enrich them. It had no other basis to exist. In the civil war, Bashar and his government decimated the entire country and reduced it to among the weakest societies in the world just so that his family could maintain their grip on power. A similar analysis can be made for the dictatorships that existed in Iraq, Libya, and elsewhere. This was what nationalism and secularism gifted the Middle East: vanity. And truly, it wasted a century.

However, the truly most devastating failure of Arab nationalism was indeed 1967 and the war with Israel. Israel's six-day lightning capture of the West Bank, the Sinai, the

Golan, and of course East Jerusalem was a humiliating disaster for Arab nationalists and exposed the weaknesses of their regimes. The war demonstrated that Arab nationalist states were not only incapable of uniting, but also incapable of defending themselves effectively against external threats due to their inability to cooperate.

Ultimately, Arab nationalism, instead of fostering economic growth, political stability, or even just military strength, left the Middle East in a worse place than where it began. As a matter of fact, nations that completely abstained from entangling themselves in the movement, such as Saudi Arabia, UAE, Qatar, and rest of the Gulf, emerged far more prosperous than those that welcomed the nationalist wave into its political spaces. The failure to establish a coherent national identity, coupled with unrealistic ambitions of unity, left the Arab world weaker, divided, and struggling with the same issues that in some ways continue to plague it to this very day.

Today, the legacy of Arab nationalism continues to weigh heavily on the region, but now only as a relic of the past. In December 2024, the Syrian regime of Bashar Al-Assad, the last Arab nationalist government, fell to the opposition forces of Idlib. With the liberation of Damascus, the last remnants of that nationalist era fell alongside the fallen regime. Moving forward, Arab nations, most especially the new Syria, must abandon such outdated political identities and focus on practical governance, economic development, and regional cooperation above all else. Only by learning from past mistakes and failures of the 20th century can the Arab world and Syria, most of all, begin to chart a new path toward the stability, progress, and perhaps even the unity that the people have been seeking for so long.

But above all else, leadership, rooted in the teachings of the Quran and the Sunnah, must be taken as the model by the new Syrian leaders. Secularism, in its nature, is devoid of an adherence to justice. Tearing Islam and every political and social tradition upheld by it, from the heart of the state, leaves it without Suleiman's justice, Mehmed's tolerance, and Salahuddin's mercy. None of this calls for a strict or radical implementation of Islam in the political space, such as what has been seen with the Taliban in Afghanistan or worse with Ayatollah-ruled Iran. Rather, the justice that is exemplified in the Quran and the Sunnah, which place the greatest emphasis on mercy, tolerance, and forgiveness, are the basis of a state's governance.

Ibn Taymiyyah famously stated, "Allah supports the just state even if it is non-Muslim, and He does not support the unjust state even if it is Muslim."

Within the Islamic tradition, the demand for justice is made as a clear and fundamental principle for true leadership. The caliphate, in name, is not leadership. The exemplification of the justice of the Quran and the Sunnah *is*. When this story first began with Jerusalem falling to the First Crusade in 1099, the Muslims were initially paralyzed from taking any serious action against these clear atrocities. For over 80 years, a man could be born and would die without there ever being a free Al-Aqsa. That changed with the generation of Salahuddin, when there was true leadership along with support from the people, enabling the change to finally come not through the caliphate but simply through a just leader and a group of skilled, driven, united, and supportive individuals beside him.

Before Sultan Salahuddin and the era of revival, the Abbasid caliph in Baghdad was rendered incapacitated in the affairs of the Muslims. He was pathetically unable to even try to take action against the Crusaders, leaving the Muslims with a weak and careless man as a mere figurehead and a complete non-player in world affairs. Once the Ummah realized this lesson, were they able to understand that they did not need a caliphate to free themselves from decline and set themselves on the path of revival.

When Al-Aqsa was finally recaptured in 1187, it was not having the caliphate that made this possible, but it was having true leadership, which at its core, was the justice and mercy of Islam. Salahuddin's generation proved that the success of revival will only come to a people once they have a generation that stands ready with unwavering faith to prevail and to conquer; not simply lands, but hearts with the morals of the faith they carry before the world.

"And when they became steadfast and believed in Our revelations, we appointed from among them leaders, who guided by Our command."

وَجَعَلْنَا مِنْهُمْ أَئِمَّةً يَهْدُونَ بِأَمْرِنَا لَمَّا صَبَرُوا وَكَانُوا بِـَٔايَٰتِنَا يُوقِنُونَ

- Surah As-Sajdah of the Quran (32:24)

Appendix

Text References

- "A Line in the Sand: Britain, France, and the Struggle that Shaped the Middle East" by James Barr
  - *Barr, James. A Line in the Sand: Britain, France, and the Struggle that Shaped the Middle East.* New York: Simon & Schuster, 2011.
- "Bible and Sword: England and Palestine from the Bronze Age to Balfour" by Barbara W. Tuchman
  - *Tuchman, Barbara W. Bible and Sword: England and Palestine from the Bronze Age to Balfour.* New York: New York University Press, 1956.
- "From Istanbul to Haifa" by Ammar Sinan
  - *Sinan, Ammar. From Istanbul to Haifa.* [Publisher info not available—please provide publisher and year for a complete citation.]
- "Saladin: The Triumph of the Sunni Revival" by Dr. A. R. Azzam
  - *Azzam, A. R. Saladin: The Triumph of the Sunni Revival.* Cambridge, MA: Harvard University Press, 2007.
- "The Life of Saladin" by Baha ad-Din Ibn Shaddad
  - *Ibn Shaddad, Baha ad-Din. The Life of Saladin.* Translated by C. W. Wilson. London:

Committee of the Palestine Exploration Fund, 1897.
- ❖ "The Crusades Through Arab Eyes" by Amin Maalouf
  - ➢ *Maalouf, Amin. The Crusades Through Arab Eyes.* Translated by Jon Rothschild. New York: Schocken Books, 1984.

Image References

- ❖ 1154 Map of the World
  - ➢ Muhammad Al-Idrisi. Tabula Rogeriana. 1154. Manuscript map. Palermo, Sicily, Italy.
- ❖ 1537 Ottoman Painting of Istanbul
  - ➢ Matrakçı Nasuh. *Ottoman Painting of Istanbul.* 1537. Manuscript illustration. Istanbul University Library, Turkey.
- ❖ 1555 Map of Cairo by Piri Reis
  - ➢ Piri Reis. *Map of Cairo.* c.1555. Manuscript map. Topkapi Palace Museum Library, Istanbul, Turkey.
- ❖ 16th-century Ottoman Painting of Aleppo

- ➢ Matrakçı Nasuh. *Ottoman Painting of Aleppo*. 16th century. Manuscript illustration. Istanbul University Library, Turkey.
- ❖ 16th-century Turkish Cavalry Armor (Museum of Islamic Art in Doha, Qatar)
  - ➢ *Armor for a Horse and Rider from Turkey*. 16th century. Museum of Islamic Art, Doha, Qatar.
- ❖ 16th-century Turkish Cavalry Armor (The Louvre Abu Dhabi, UAE)
  - ➢ *Ottoman Armor of a Rider and a Horse*. 16th century. Collection of the Louvre Abu Dhabi, United Arab Emirates.
- ❖ 19th-century Ottoman Drawing of Masjid Al-Aqsa
  - ➢ [Artist unknown]. *Ottoman Drawing of Al-Aqsa Mosque*. 19th century. Ottoman Empire.
- ❖ 19th-century Ottoman Painting of Masjid An-Nabawi
  - ➢ [Artist unknown]. *Ottoman Painting of the Prophet's Mosque*. 19th century. Ottoman Empire.
- ❖ 19th-century Ottoman Painting of Mecca

- ➤ [Artist unknown]. *Ottoman Painting of Mecca.* 19th century. Ottoman Empire.
- ❖ Coin of Guy de Lusignan, Kingdom of Cyprus (1192 - 1194)
  - ➤ [Anonymous]. *Coin of Guy de Lusignan.* 1192–1194. Kingdom of Cyprus.
- ❖ Coin of Richard I, Duke of Aquitaine (1172 - 1189)
  - ➤ [Anonymous]. *Coin of Richard I of Aquitaine.* 1172–1189. France.
- ❖ Dinar of Salahuddin (1184)
  - ➤ [Anonymous]. *Dinar of Salahuddin.* 1184. Ayyubid Dynasty.
- ❖ Dirhams of Salahuddin (1182 - 1183, 1182 - 1183, 1190 - 1191, 1215 - 1216)
  - ➤ [Anonymous]. *Dirham of Salahuddin.* Various Mints, Ayyubid Dynasty.
- ❖ Map of Acre by Bosio, Giacomo, & Pierre de Boissat (1659)
  - ➤ Bosio, Giacomo, and Pierre de Boissat. *Map of Acre.* 1659. From *Guerres sacrées et croissades.* Paris, France.

- Map of the Salahuddin's Dominion
    - [Anonymous]. *Map of Salahuddin's Dominion.* October 7, 2010.
- Old City of Damascus Oil Painting
    - Syrian School. *View of the city of Damascus.* 17th century. Popular Traditions Museum, Damascus, Syria.
- Penny of Richard I (1189 - 1199)
    - [Anonymous]. *Penny of Richard I.* 1189–1199. England, UK.
- Siege Towers, Cassell's Illustrated Universal History, 1883
    - Cassell and Company. *Siege Towers.* In *Cassell's Illustrated Universal History*, vol. 2. London: Cassell & Co., 1883.
- Sword of the Prophet Muhammad ﷺ, Topkapi Palace, Istanbul, Turkey
    - [Anonymous]. *Sword of the Prophet Muhammad ﷺ.* Topkapi Palace Museum, Istanbul, Turkey.
- The *Shalandi*, an 11th-century Arab Warship

➤ [Artist unknown]. *The Shalandi – Arab Warship*. 11th century. Illustration.

❖ Zengid Dirham from Sinjar (1210 - 1211)

➤ [Anonymous]. *Dirham, Zengid Dynasty (Sinjar)*. 1210–1211. Iraq.

Made in the USA
Coppell, TX
08 May 2025

49113679R00154